Keto Diet Bread

The Complete Guide for Low-Carb Recipes Don't Give Up on Taste

You Lose Weight by Eating Healthy

Pauly Brown

Table of contest

Introduction ix

Chapter 1: Foods on the Ketogenic Diet Plan 1

Bulletproof Coffee 1

Make Your Homemade Pumpkin Pie Spice: 7

Chapter 2: Healthy Bread Choices 12

Almond Bread 12

Cheesy Italian Baked Bread 13

Cheesy Skillet Bread..15

Coconut Bread..16

Delicious Collagen Keto Bread...................................17

Flaxseed Bread with Coconut Flour.............................18

Garlic Bread...19

Gluten-Free Bread.. 20

Heavenly Cloud Bread...21

Keto Bread Loaves 22

Macadamia Bread 23

Microwave Bread - Almond Flour 24

Microwave Bread - Coconut Flour 25

Soft Keto Seed Bread.. 26

Soul Bread 27

Spring Onion Bread 28

Tasty Cottage Bread 29

Chapter 3: Delicious Muffins 30

Cheese Muffins 30

Cheeseburger Muffins 31

English Muffins 32

1-Minute Muffin 33

Pesto Egg Muffins 34

Squash Muffins 35

Sweet Muffins 36

Almond & Apple Muffins 36

Apple Cinnamon Muffins 37

Blueberry Flaxseed Muffins 38

Brownie Muffins 39

Cinnamon & Apple Spiced Muffins 40

Cinnamon & Applesauce Muffins 41

Lemon Coconut Muffins 42

Lemon Poppyseed Muffins 43

Pumpkin Muffins 44

Pumpkin Maple Flaxseed Muffins 45

Unflavored Coconut Flour Muffins 47

Delicious Bagels 48

Almond Mozzarella Bagels 48

Bagels with Cheese 49

Cinnamon Raisin Bagels 50

Garlic Coconut Flour – Gluten-Free Bagels 51

Homemade Croissant Bagels 52

Onion Bagels – Gluten-Free 53

Pumpkin Bagels.. 54

Sesame & Poppy Seed Bagels 56

Chapter 4: Ketogenic Buns - Biscuits & Rolls........ 57

Buns 57

Almond Buns for Sandwiches 57

Basil Buns.. 58

Breakfast Buns 59

Burger Buns.. 60

Hot Dog Buns - Almond Flour 61

Hot Dog Deluxe Buns 62

Italian Seasoning Buns.................................. 63

Poppy Seed Buns 64

Protein Buns... 65

Sesame Buns 66

Spring Onion Buns 67

Swedish Keto Buns 68

Tahini Hamburger Buns 69

Biscuits 70

Almond Flour Biscuits 70

Biscuits & Gravy 72

Buttery Garlic & Sharp Cheddar Biscuits 73

Cheddar Bay Biscuits 74

Lavender Biscuits..75

30-Minute Drop Biscuits 76

Tomato & Zucchini Biscuits 78

White Cheddar Sausage Breakfast Biscuits 79

Rolls 80

    Coconut Flour Rolls 80

    Dinner Rolls 81

    Fathead Rolls 82

    Fiber Bread Rolls 83

    Garlic Parmesan Knots 84

    Keto Bread Rolls 86

    Keto - Paleo Dinner Rolls 88

    Low-Carb Cream Cheese Rolls 89

    Oopsie Rolls 90

    Rosemary Rolls 91

Chapter 5: Ketogenic Sandwiches 92

  Bread for Sandwiches 92

    Cheese Flatbread.. 92

    Delicious Flatbread.. 93

    Focaccia Bread 94

    Keto Naan Bread 95

    Pita Bread 97

  Other Sandwiches 98

    Keto Grilled Cheese Sandwiches 98

    90-Second Bread with Almond Flour................100

    Pancake Sandwich 101

    Ingredients Needed - The Filling: 101

Chapter 6: Ketogenic Sweet Bread 103

  Banana Bread...103

  Blueberry English Muffin Bread Loaf 104

  Chocolate Zucchini Bread...............................105

Cinnamon Almond Flour Bread..................................107

Cranberry Bread - Gluten-Free................................ 108

Italian Christmas Bread - Gluten-Free 109

Lemon & Blueberry Bread 111

Low-Carb Chocolate Loaf.. 112

Peanut Butter Berry Breakfast Loaf.......................... 113

Pumpkin Bread 114

Seedy Pumpkin Bread... 115

Slow-Cooked Gingerbread 117

Slow-Cooked Zucchini Bread...................................118

Chapter 7: Ketogenic Cookies...............................119

Amaretti Cookies.. 119

Chocolate Chip Cookies... 120

Chocolate Coconut Cookies..................................... 121

Cinnamon Cookies 122

Ginger Snap Cookies 123

Graham Crackers...124

Macaroons 125

Orange Walnut Cookies 126

P B & J Cookies 127

Pistachio Cookies 128

Walnut Cookies 129

Conclusion... 130

Hot Chocolate... 131

Introduction

Congratulations on downloading your personal copy of the *Keto Diet Bread*. Thank you for doing so. If you are expecting a lot of delicious bread options, you have come to the right place. You will have a huge variety of bread to fill your bread cravings with plenty of delicious sweet bread for breakfast, too. First, let's discover a bit about the keto plan.

During the Paleogenic period, humans were known to hunt for their protein and gather their vegetables, fruits, nuts, and seeds to survive. Because this method isn't ideal in today's society; you don't have to search for food each day. That was the way people lived centuries ago, which made the body develop a survival mechanism to survive during times when food was scarce. Whenever a person encountered satiation, where they consumed more calories than they burned, the unused calories would be converted into fat fuels and stored for emergency starvation times.

However, in modern times, food is not only natural to come by, but many meals that are affordable are packed full of unnecessary calories. Your body will continue to create these fat stores, even though the times of hunting and gathering are behind us. These facts were taken into consideration when the ketogenic diet was developed.

The ketogenic diet or keto diet plan is a low-carbohydrate and high-fat system. It provides satisfactory levels of protein, which is similar to other low-carbohydrate diets. Ketosis is a process that occurs every day, no matter what or how many carbs you consume. The superior keto plan speeds up the process with a standard and safe chemical reaction.

The methods used will reduce your body's carbohydrate intake drastically as it is replaced with fat. Your body goes into ketosis, which is a metabolic state making your body burn fat for energy. Your brain can also receive energy—transported as ketones from the liver when fat is exchanged. Your body also produces insulin and blood sugar/glucose when you eat foods high in carbohydrates; which as a result, are also lowered on the ketogenic diet.

The plan maintains adequate amounts of protein so your body can repair and regain a healthy status. The diet will also supply you with the calories needed to keep a healthy weight for your height and age. Let's see what is allowed on the plan!

Chapter 1: Foods on the Ketogenic Diet Plan

Before we begin, why not try a delicious cup of coffee? Here's the recipe:

Bulletproof Coffee

Yields: 1 Serving

Total Macros: 463 Calories| -0- g Net Carbs |1 g Protein | 51 g Total Fats

Ingredients Needed:

- MCT oil powder (2 tbsp.)
- Ghee or butter (2 tbsp.)
- Hot coffee (1.5 cups)

Preparation Instructions:

1. Empty the hot coffee into your blender.
2. Pour in the powder and butter. Blend until frothy.
3. Enjoy in a large mug.

Before You Get Started:

Gather the Right Accessories for Baking

A Good Set of Scales*:* Portion control is essential for baking bread. You want a scale that will accommodate your needs. Consider these options:

Removable Plate: Keep the germs off of the scale by removing the plate. Be sure it will come off to eliminate the bacterial buildup.

- *Seek A Conversion Button:* You need to know how to convert measurements into grams since not all recipes have them listed. The grams keep the system in complete harmony.

- *The Tare Function:* When you set a bowl on the scale, the feature will allow you to reset the scale back to zero.

Accurate Measuring Tools*:* A measuring cup and spoon system that shows both the Metric and US standards of weight is essential, so there is no confusion during prep. If you are stocking your kitchen for baking, it's also essential to choose a clear container where you can see the contents.

Sifter*:* Purchase a good sifter for under $10, and you will be ensured a more accurate measurement for your baking needs.

Parchment paper will be used for most of the bread recipes. The baking pans are lined with the paper and the baked goods do not stick. For most baking needs, you can omit the oils if you choose the paper instead. However, some recipes use paper and oils.

Immersion or Regular Blender & Food Processor: These are useful for many stages of bread preparation.

Low-Carb Choices of Flour

- **Coconut Flour:** Each 1/4 cup of coconut flour contains 7 grams of net carbs and 2.5 grams of fat. It displays that tropical taste. Be sure it's stored in a closed container. Choose a spot where it's dark such as the pantry. The refrigerator and freezer could cause moisture contamination.

- **Almond Flour:** Almond flour is more of all-purpose flour and only contains 3 grams of carbs for 1/4 of a cup. (In comparison, totals are overwhelming for the regular wheat flour at 24 grams. That's why it is not on your diet plan.) Almonds are blanched in boiling water to remove the skins and then ground into fine flour used for baking low-carb cakes, cookies, and pie crusts.

- **Almond Meal:** Almond meal isn't the same as almond flour. However, if you're running low on almond flour for baked goods like muffins and cookies, then merely throw some almonds in a food processor to make a substitute for the meal. The texture is a little different than flour, but the baking results are the same. Almond meal contains 11.1 carbs and 48.2 fat in 100 grams (about 7/8 of a cup).

- **Egg White Protein Powder:** Try adding the protein powder to provide more elasticity to gluten when you're making bread. The powder will also add more protein to your diet counts.

- **Sesame Flour:** Finely grind sesame seeds to prepare the flour into a texture similar to wheat flour. Combine with psyllium flour for your baking needs to ensure the light texture of high-carb white bread.

- **Pumpkin Seed Meal:** You can process raw or toasted pumpkin seeds to make a thick meal. One cup of seeds has 3 net carbs and 12 grams of fat.

- **Whole Psyllium Husk:** Use the entire husk in the dough where you require more stretchiness, such as what you would have in wheat flour. It's excellent for pizza dough, tortillas, or bread.

- **Psyllium Husk Powder:** Fiber is its main ingredient but it's also combined with other low-carb flowers. You'll need to add plenty of liquids to your baking items such as muffins or bread.

Keto-Friendly Sweeteners

- **Stevia Drops** include English toffee, hazelnut, vanilla, and chocolate flavors. Stevia is a common herb known as sugar leaf and is available in drops, glycerite, or in powder form. Enjoy making a satisfying cup of sweetened coffee or other favorite drink. Some individuals think the stevia drops are too bitter. At first, use only three drops to equal one teaspoon of sugar.

- ***Xylitol*** is at the top of the sugary list. It tastes just like sugar! The natural-occurring sugar alcohol has the Glycemic index (GI) standing of 13. If you have tried others and weren't satisfied, this might be for you. Xylitol is also known to help keep mouth bacteria in check, which goes a long way to protect your dental health. The ingredient is commonly found in chewing gum. Unfortunately, if used in large amounts, it can cause diarrhea - making chewing gum a laxative. *Pet Warning*: If you have a puppy in the house, be sure to use caution since it is toxic to dogs (even small amounts).

- ***Swerve Granular Sweetener*** is also an excellent choice as a blend. It's made from non-digestible carbs sourced from starchy root veggies and select fruits. Start with 3/4 of a teaspoon for every one of sugar. Increase the portion to your liking. Swerve also has its own confectioners or powdered sugar for your baking needs. On the downside, it is more expensive.

- ***Pyure's Organic All-Purpose Blend*** is considered the best all-around sweetener. The blend of stevia and erythritol is an excellent alternative to baking, sweetening desserts, and various cooking needs. The substitution ratio is one teaspoon of sugar for each one-third teaspoon of Pyure. Add slowly and adjust to your taste since you can always add a bit more.

  Note: If you need powdered sugar, just grind the Pyure sweetener in a NutriBullet or high-speed blender until it's very dry.

- ***Sorbitol*** is sugar alcohol manufactured from cornstarch which can be used in powder form to withstand high temperatures.

- ***Coconut sugar*** is much lower than table sugar with 15 calories or 4 grams of carbs per teaspoon.

The list of sweeteners listed has a glycemic index rating next to them. This is a measurement of how much your blood sugar is raised after you consume a specific food. If there is a zero (0) next to it; that means it will not increase your blood sugar counts. The measurement can reach 100 which is the baseline of insulin.

- Stevia liquid - GI: 0
- Erythritol - GI: 0
- Aspartame – GI: 0
- Monk Fruit GI: 0
- Inulin – GI: 0
- Xylitol- GI: 13
- Sucralose (liquid) GI: Variable
- Maltitol – GI: 36
- Saccharin – GI: Variable

Choose Healthy Fats & Oils

Use Extra-Virgin Olive Oil (EVOO): Olive oil dates back for centuries – back to where oil was used for anointing kings and priests. High-quality oil with its low-acidity makes the oil have a smoke point as high as 410° Fahrenheit. That's higher than most cooking applications call for, making olive oil more heat-stable than many other cooking fats. It contains (2 tsp.) -0- carbs.

Mono-unsaturated fats, such as the ones in olive oil, are also linked with better blood sugar regulation, including lower fasting glucose, as well as reducing inflammation throughout the body. Olive oil also helps to prevent cardiovascular disease by protecting the integrity of your vascular system and lowering LDL which is also called the 'bad' cholesterol.

Use Coconut Oil: You vamp up your fat intake with this high flash-point oil. Enjoy a coconut oil smoothie before your workouts. Use it with your meats, chicken, fish, or on top of veggies. It will quickly transfer from solid form to oil according to its temperature.

Use Macadamia Oil: One of the benefits of this oil is that it has a high smoke point. It carries a mild flavor which is a super alternative to olive oil in mayonnaise.

Choose the Best Spices

Make Your Homemade Pumpkin Pie Spice:

Use this simple low-carb concoction, and you know it will be healthy.
Yields: 10.75 tsp. @ 1 tsp. per serving
Macros: 0.8 g Net Carbs| 6.42 Calories| 0.12 g Protein| 0.09 g Total Fats

What You Need:

- Cinnamon (2 tbsp.)
- Allspice (.5 tsp.)
- Nutmeg (.5 tsp.)
- Ground ginger (1 tbsp.
- Cardamom (.25 tsp.)
- Ground cloves (.5 tsp.) or (.75 tsp.) whole cloves

How to Prepare:

1. Use a spice grinder to grind the cloves into powder.
2. Combine all of the components into a large mixing container until combined thoroughly.
3. Store in a spice container to use any time the need arises.

Choose Healthy Nuts & Seeds:

You can choose from an array of nuts in moderation. The number of carbs represents the net carbs which equal approximately 3.5 ounces:

- Chia Seeds -0- grams
- Flax seeds -0- grams
- Brazil nuts – 4 grams
- Pecans – 4 grams
- Macadamia – 5 grams
- Hazelnuts – 7 grams
- Peanuts – 7 grams
- Walnuts – 7 grams
- Peanuts – 7 grams
- Pine Nuts – 9 grams
- Almonds – 10 grams
- Pumpkin seeds – 14.3 grams
- Sesame seeds – 17.7 grams
- Pistachios – 18 grams

In comparison, you now see why those potato chips are 48 grams and M&Ms are 70 grams.

List of Keto-Friendly Veggies

You can enjoy veggies any time of day. Each of these has the Net Carbs listed per 100 grams or 1/2 cup:

- Alfalfa Seeds – Sprouted - 0.2
- Arugula – 2.05
- Asparagus – 1.78
- Bamboo shoots: 3
- Beans – Green snap – 3.6
- Beet greens – 0.63
- Bell pepper
- Broccoli – 4.04
- Broccoli raab – 0.15

- Carrots – 6.78
- Carrots – baby – 5.34
- Cauliflower – 2.97
- Celery – 1.37
- Chard – 2.14
- Chicory greens – 0.7
- Chives – 1.85
- Coriander – Cilantro Leaves – 0.87
- Cucumber with Peel – 3.13
- Eggplant – 2.88
- Garlic – 30.96
- Ginger root – 15.77
- Kale – 5.15
- Leeks – bulb (+) lower leaf – 12.35
- Lemongrass – citronella 25.31
- Lettuce – red leaf – 1.36
- Lettuce – crisphead types - ex. iceberg 1.77
- Mushrooms brown – 3.7
- Mustard Greens – 1.47
- Onions – yellow – 7.64
- Onions – scallions or spring – 4.74
- Onions – sweet – 6.65
- Peppers – banana – 1.95
- Peppers – red hot chili – 7.31
- Peppers – jalapeno – 3.7
- Peppers – sweet – green – 2.94
- Peppers – sweet – red – 3.93
- Peppers – sweet – yellow – 5.42
- Portabella Mushrooms – 2.57
- Pumpkin – 6
- Radishes – 1.8
- Seaweed – kelp – 8.27
- Seaweed – spirulina - 2.02
- Shiitake mushrooms – 4.29
- Spinach – 1.43
- Squash 0 crookneck, summer – 2.64
- Squash - Zucchini – 2.11
- Squash – winter – acorn – 8.92

- Tomatoes – 2.69
- Turnips – 4.63
- Turnip Greens – 3.93
- White Mushrooms – 2.26

List of Keto-Friendly Fruits

Fruits are excellent snack foods. Each of the following is portioned for .5 cup servings or 100 grams:

- Apples – no skin - boiled – 13.6 total carbs
- Apricots - 7.5 total carbs
- Bananas - 23.4 total carbs
- Fresh Blackberries - 5.4 net carbs
- Fresh Blueberries - 8.2 net carbs
- Fresh Strawberries - 3 net carbs
- Cantaloupe - 6 total carbs
- Raw Cranberries - 4 net carbs
- Gooseberries - 8.8 net carbs
- Kiwi – 14.2 total carbs
- Fresh Boysenberries - 8.8 net carbs
- Oranges – 11.7 total carbs
- Peaches - 11.6 total carbs
- Pears – 19.2 total carbs
- Pineapple - 11 total carbs
- Plums – 16.3 total carbs
- Watermelon- 7.1 total carbs

Now that you have the main idea of what the diet supports, now, it's time to see how to prepare the delicious bread options of choice.

Chapter 2: Healthy Bread Choices

Almond Bread

Yields: 4 Servings
Total Macros: 2 g Net Carbs | 8 g Total Protein |
24 g Total Fats | 257 Calories

Ingredients Needed:

- Almond flour (1 cup)
- Eggs (2 whisked)
- Baking powder (1.5 tsp.)
- Olive oil (3 tbsp.)
- *Also Needed*: 3.5 x 8-inch baking pan

[handwritten: ADD SALT]
[handwritten: 2 t. SWEETNER]

Preparation Instructions:

1. Warm up the oven to reach 350° Fahrenheit.
2. Grease the baking pan.
3. Combine all of the components to form a sticky dough.
4. Arrange in the greased tin and bake for 30 minutes.
5. Carefully remove the bread and slice into four squares, similar to flatbread.

Cheesy Italian Baked Bread

Yields: 4 Servings
Total Macros: 2.59g Net Carbs | 21.7 g Total Fats|
16.5 g Protein | 277 Calories

Ingredients Needed:

- Coconut flour (4 tbsp.)
- Flaxseed meal (3 tbsp.)
- Italian seasoning (1 tsp.)
- Shredded Monterey jack cheese (1.25 cups)
- Egg (1 large)
- Egg yolk (1 large)
- Olive oil (1 tsp.)
- Provolone cheese (28 grams – 4 slices)
- Italian dry salami (4 small slices)
- Fresh spinach leaves (1 oz.)
- Deli sliced mild pepper rings (.25 cup)
- *Also Needed*: Rolling pin

Preparation Instructions:

1. Warm up the oven to reach 400° Fahrenheit.
2. Combine the Italian seasoning, flaxseed meal, and coconut flour.
3. In another dish, melt the Monterey jack cheese in the microwave until the shreds are fully melted (1 min.). Let it set for one minute and add the cheese with the whole egg. Mix well. Fold in the dry fixings until it's all mixed.
4. Spread out the dough on a layer of parchment paper and one on top of the dough. Roll it out where one side is wide enough for the fillings. (Braid on the other side.)
5. Portion the salami and provolone cheese.
6. Next, just tear the spinach to place on top with a layer of the pepper rings, and a spritz of the oil.

7. Slice the sides of the dough into strips (for braiding) using a pizza cutter or sharp knife.
8. Fold-in each end of the bread. Braid the sliced strips on each side.
9. Whisk one of the egg yolks to brush across the top.
10. Bake for 15 to 18 minutes. Serve.

Cheesy Skillet Bread

Yields: 10 Servings
Total Macros: 3 g Net Carbs |12.5 g Total Protein|
31 g Total Fats | 357 Calories

Ingredients Needed:

- Butter for the skillet (1 tbsp.)
- Almond flour (2 cups)
- Salt (.5 tsp.)
- Flaxseed meal (.5 cup)
- Baking powder (2 tsp.)
- Shredded Cheddar cheese divided (1.5 cups)
- Eggs - lightly beaten (3 large)
- Melted butter (.5 cup)
- Almond milk (.75 cup)

Preparation Instructions:

1. Warm up the oven to reach 425° Fahrenheit.
2. Melt the butter in a 10-inch ovenproof skillet in the oven.
3. Whisk the almond flour, flaxseed meal, baking powder, salt, and 1 cup of the shredded cheese.
4. Stir in the melted butter, eggs, and almond milk until thoroughly combined.
5. Remove the hot skillet from oven, and swirl butter to coat the sides.
6. Empty the batter into the pan. Sprinkle with rest of the cheddar.
7. Bake until browned around the edges and set through the middle (approximately 16 to 20 minutes).
8. The cheese on top should be nicely browned. Transfer to the countertop to cool for 15 minutes before serving.

Coconut Bread

Yields: 8 Servings
Total Macros: 3.8 g Net Carbs |154 Calories|9.2 g Protein |
5 g Total Fats

Ingredients Needed:

- Flaxseed meal (.5 cup)
- Baking soda (.5 tsp.)
- Sifted coconut flour (1 cup)
- Baking powder (1 tsp.)
- Salt (1 tsp.)
- Apple cider vinegar (1 tbsp.)
- Water (.5 cup)
- Room temperature eggs(6 large)

Preparation Instructions:

1. Warm up the oven in advance to 350° Fahrenheit.
2. Lightly grease the baking pan of choice.
3. Sift the flour into a mixing container. Fold in the remainder of the dry fixings. Mix well.
4. Pour in the vinegar and water to form a thick batter. Press into the prepared pan/pans.
5. Bake until browned or for approximately 40 minutes.
6. Cool in the pan until slightly warm and remove. Slice and serve.

Delicious Collagen Keto Bread

Yields: 12 Slices
Total Macros: 77 Calories| -0- g Net Carbs |7 g Protein |
5 g Total Fats

Ingredients Needed:

- Unflavored Grass-Fed Collagen Protein (.5 cup)
- Almond flour (6 tbsp.)
- Pastured eggs - separated (5)
- Unflavored liquid coconut oil - butter or ghee (1 tbsp.) or parchment paper (trimmed to fit the dish)
- Himalayan pink salt (1 pinch)
- Baking powder (1 tsp.)
- Xanthan gum (1 tsp.)
- *Optional*: Stevia (1 pinch)
- *Also Needed*: 1.5-quart glass or ceramic loaf dish

Preparation Instructions:

1. Warm up the oven to 325° Fahrenheit.
2. Generously oil (*only*) the bottom part of the loaf dish with coconut oil.
3. Whisk the whites of the eggs to form stiff peaks. Put them to the side for now.
4. Whisk the dry fixings. (Add the optional pinch of stevia if desired.)
5. Whisk together the wet fixings; liquid coconut oil and egg yolks. Set aside.
6. Combine it all well. The batter will be thick and gooey. Dump it into the baking dish.
7. Prepare in the heated oven for 40 minutes.
8. Transfer from the oven. Let it cool for one to two hours.
9. Once the bread is cooled, release the loaf from the pan using a knife around the edges of the dish.
10. Slice into when ready to use.

Flaxseed Bread with Coconut Flour

Yields: 8 Servings
Total Macros: 183 Calories| 3 g Net Carbs | 0 Protein |
14 g Total Fats

Ingredients Needed:

- Water (10 tbsp.)
- Coconut flour (.75 cup)
- Ground flaxseed or flax meal (.5 cup)
- Large eggs (3 whole + 3 whites)
- Olive oil (5 tbsp.)
- Sea salt (1 pinch)
- Baking powder (2 tsp.)

Preparation Instructions:

1. Warm up the oven to 350° Fahrenheit.
2. Spritz a bread pan with cooking oil, greasing well.
3. Mix the egg whites and eggs with a processor or electric mixer until foamy. Add the remainder of the fixings. Work the dough until it's smooth.
4. Let the dough rest for 4 to 5 minutes so the flax and coconut flours can absorb the moisture.
5. Add to the prepared pan and bake until the top is browned (approximately 35 minutes). If you bake the bread as a loaf, you need to increase the cooking time by 10 minutes. (Muffins – 25 to 30 min.)
6. *Cooking Tip*: This loaf is excellent when prepared using a silicone loaf mold.

Garlic Bread

Yields: 20 Servings
Total Macros: 92 Calories| 1 g Net Carbs| 9 g Total Fats |
2 g Total Protein

Ingredients Needed:

- Baking powder (2 tsp.)
- Almond flour (1.25 cups)
- Ground psyllium husk powder (5 tbsp.)
- Sea salt (1 tsp.)
- White wine or cider vinegar (2 tsp.)
- Boiling water (1 cup)
- Egg whites (3)

Fixings Needed - Garlic Butter:

- Butter - room temperature (4 oz.)
- Garlic clove (1 minced)
- Fresh parsley - finely chopped (2 tbsp.)
- Salt (.5 tsp.)

Preparation Method:

1. Warm up the oven to reach 350° Fahrenheit.
2. Combine the dry fixings in a mixing container.
3. Start the pot of water. Once boiling, pour in the egg whites and vinegar. Whisk using a hand mixer for about 30 seconds.
4. Shape and roll into garlic bread buns, leaving plenty of space for expansion.
5. Bake using the lower rack for 40 to 50 minutes. When ready, remove to cool.
6. Prepare the garlic butter and chill.
7. Take the garlic butter out of the fridge. Slice the cooled buns using a serrated knife. Spread garlic butter on each half.
8. Reheat the oven to 425° Fahrenheit.
9. Bake until lightly browned (10 to 15 min.).

Gluten-Free Bread

Yields: 8 Slices
Total Macros: 3 g Net Carbs |267 Calories|
9 g Total Protein | 24 g Total Fats

Ingredients Needed:

- Salt (.25 tsp.)
- Coconut flour (2 tbsp.)
- Baking soda (1.5 tsp.)
- Flaxseed meal (.25 cup)
- Almond flour (1.5 cups)
- Eggs (5)
- Coconut oil (.25 cup)
- Honey or substitute (1 tsp.)
- Apple cider vinegar (1 tbsp.)

Preparation Instructions:

1. Set the oven temperature to 350° Fahrenheit.
2. Lightly spritz a loaf pan with cooking oil spray.
3. Mix the flaxseed, salt, baking soda, almond flour, and coconut flour in a food processor. Pulse and pour in the vinegar, oil, and eggs. Pulse and add to the prepared pan.
4. Bake for 1/2 of an hour. Transfer to the counter for ten minutes in the pan.
5. Place on a wire rack and finish cooling before storing.

Heavenly Cloud Bread

Yields: 8 Servings
Total Macros: 122 Calories| -0- g Net Carbs |
7 g Total Protein |10 g Total Fats

Ingredients Needed:

- Eggs (3)
- Room temperature cream cheese (3 tbsp.)
- Baking powder (.5 tsp.)
- Salt (as desired)

Preparation Instructions:

1. Separate the egg yolks and whip the whites with the salt and cream cheese.
2. In another dish, whip the baking powder with the egg yolks. Stir together.
3. Warm up the oven to reach 300° Fahrenheit.
4. Line a baking pan with a sheet of the parchment paper.
5. Scoop the dough into the prepared pan – leaving spaces between each one.
6. Bake for 15 to 20 minutes and enjoy the clouds.

oaves

Servings
Macros: 3 g Net Carbs| 134 Calories|8.2 g Total
in |8.3 g Total Fats

What You Need:

- Large eggs - room temperature (6)
- Coconut flour - sifted (1 cup)
- Baking soda (.5 tsp.)
- Flaxseed meal (.5 cup)
- Salt (1 tsp.)
- Baking powder (1 tsp.)
- Water (.5 cup)
- Apple cider vinegar (1 tbsp.)
- Also Needed: 2 loaf pans

Preparation Instructions:

1. Warm up the oven to reach 350° Fahrenheit.
2. Grease the pans and sift the coconut flour into a container. Combine with the remainder of the dry components and whisk.
3. Stir in the vinegar, water, and eggs. Once it's thick, add the batter to the prepared pans.
4. Bake for 40 minutes and cool in the pan until warm. Remove from the pans and serve.

Macadamia Bread

Yields: 16 Servings
Total Macros: 227 Calories| 5 g Net Carbs| 22 g Total Fats|
5 g Total Protein

Ingredients Needed:

- Macadamia nuts (2 cups)
- Eggs (4)
- Almond flour (.25 cup)
- Baking powder (.5 tsp.)
- Ground flaxseed (2 tbsp.)
- Softened ghee (.25 cup)
- Apple cider vinegar (2 tbsp.)
- Softened coconut butter (.5 cup)
- Sea salt (1 tsp.)
- *Also Needed*: 8 x 4 loaf pan

Preparation Instructions:

1. Warm up the oven to 350° Fahrenheit.
2. Lightly grease the pan with ghee.
3. Process the nuts using the S-blade in the food processor until they are fine flour.
4. Break the eggs and add one at a time, with the motor running until the mixture is creamy.
5. Fold in the flaxseed, almond flour, coconut butter, sea salt, ghee, vinegar, and baking powder. Once it's well combined, pour into the greased loaf pan.
6. Bake for 35 to 38 minutes.
7. Let it cool before slicing to serve or store.

Microwave Bread - Almond Flour

Yields: 2 - 4 small rounds
Total Macros: 2 g Net Carbs|3.25 g Total Protein |
13 g Total Fats | 132 Calories

Ingredients Needed:

- Almond flour (.33 cup)
- Salt (.125 tsp.)
- Baking powder (.5 tsp.)
- Melted ghee (2.5 tbsp.)
- Whisked egg (1)
- Oil (spritz for the mug)

Preparation Instructions:

1. Grease a cup with the oil. Combine all of the fixings in a mixing dish and pour into the cup. Put the cup in the microwave.
2. Set the timer using the high setting for 90 seconds.
3. Transfer the mug to a cooling space for 2 to 3 minutes. Gently remove from the mug and slice into four portions.

Microwave Bread - Coconut Flour

Yields: 4 Servings
Total Macros: 97 Calories| 1.29 g Net Carbs |2.42 g Protein |9.31 g Total Fats

Ingredients Needed:

- Coconut flour (1 tbsp.)
- Baking powder (.33 tsp.)
- Flax meal (1 tbsp.)
- Large egg (1)
- Butter (2 tbsp.)
- Parmesan cheese (1 tbsp.)
- Salt (1 pinch)

Preparation Instructions:

1. In a blender, add the eggs, melted butter, salt, baking powder, flax meal, grated parmesan, and almond flour. Blend until smooth.
2. Empty the mixture into a square container.
3. Place in the microwave for about 60 to 90 seconds.
4. Slice and cover in a closed container. Store in the freezer compartment.

Soft Keto Seed Bread

Yields: 20 Servings
Total Macros: 2 g Net Carbs | 11 g Protein | 20 g Total Fats | 223 Calories

Ingredients Needed:

- Almond flour (1 cup)
- Coconut flour (.75 cup)
- Sesame seeds (5.33 tbsp.)
- Flaxseed (.5 cup)
- Ground psyllium husk powder (.25 cup)
- Baking powder (3 tsp.)
- Ground fennel seeds or ground caraway seeds (1 tsp.)
- Salt (1 tsp.)
- Eggs (6)
- Cream cheese (7 oz.)
- Heavy whipping cream (.75 cup)
- Melted butter or melted coconut oil (.5 cup)
- *For the Topping*: Poppy seeds or sesame seeds (1 tbsp.)

Preparation Instructions:

1. Take the cream cheese from the refrigerator ahead of time to let it come to room temperature.
2. Heat up the oven to 350° Fahrenheit. Grease the baking pan or use parchment paper.
3. Incorporate all of the dry fixings in a mixing container (omit the seeds).
4. In another dish, whisk everything else until creamy smooth.
5. Place the dough into the bread pan.
6. Bake for about 45 minutes on the lower rack in the oven.
7. Take it out of the oven. Let the loaf cool on a rack.

Soul Bread

Yields: 16 Servings
Total Macros: 200 Calories| 1.1g Net Carbs | 10 g Protein | 15.2 g Total Fats

Ingredients Needed:

- Cream cheese softened (12 oz.)
- Butter (.25 cup)
- Eggs (4)
- Olive oil (.25 cup)
- Optional: Stevia drops (2 drops)
- Heavy whipping cream or Half & Half (.25 cup)
- Unflavored whey protein (1.66 cups)
- Salt (.5 tsp.)
- Cream of tartar (.25 tsp.)
- Xanthan gum (1 tsp.)
- Baking soda (.33 tsp.)
- Baking powder (2.5 tsp.)
- *Also Needed*: 9x5 bread pan or molds

Preparation Instructions:

1. Heat the oven to reach 325° Fahrenheit.
2. Prepare the pan or molds.
3. Toss the cream cheese and butter into a large microwave-safe dish.
4. Microwave for one minute.
5. Blend well using a stick blender or hand mixer.
6. Fold in the eggs, sweetener, heavy cream, and olive oil. Mix well.
7. Combine all of the dry fixings (by hand) in a separate container and add to the cream cheese mixture.
8. Scoop into the silicone mold or prepared pan.
9. Bake for about 45 minutes.
10. Let the bread cool down and wrap in plastic to store.

Spring Onion Bread

Yields: 6 Servings
Total Macros: 27 Calories| 2.2 g Total Protein|
5 g Net Carbs|1.8 g Total Fats

Ingredients Needed:

- Room temperature cream cheese (3 tbsp.)
- Separated eggs (3)
- Apple cider vinegar (1 tbsp.)
- Minced spring onions (3 tbsp.)
- Salt (as desired)

Preparation Instructions:

1. Warm up the oven to 300° Fahrenheit.
2. Whisk the egg yolks and combine with the spring onions and cream cheese.
3. In another container, whisk the salt, vinegar, and egg whites. Mix it all together.
4. Prepare in batches. Spoon the dough onto a parchment paper-lined pan. Be sure to leave room between each one.
5. Bake for 20 minutes.

Tasty Cottage Bread

Yields: 6 Servings
Total Macros: 109 Calories| 6 g Net Carbs | 8.4 g Protein | 6.3 g Total Fats

Ingredients Needed:

- Ground flaxseed (1 tsp.)
- Ground sesame seeds (1 tsp.)
- Egg (1)
- Salt (1 pinch)
- Cottage cheese (7-8 oz.)
- Turmeric powder (.125 or to taste)
- Baking powder (.5 tsp.)
- Sunflower seeds (1.5 to 2 oz.)
- Wheat bran (2 tbsp.)
- Oat bran (3 tbsp.)

Preparation Instructions:

1. Combine the sesame seeds, flaxseed, egg, and cottage cheese. Shake in the salt and turmeric. Fold in the seeds, oat bran, and wheat bran. Stir well and let the mixture rest for 10 minutes.
2. Warm up the oven to reach 425° Fahrenheit.
3. Add a sheet of parchment paper to the baking dish.
4. Wet your hands with water and shape the mixture into a ball.
5. Bake for 45 minutes in the preheated oven. Serve when ready!

Chapter 3: Delicious Muffins

Cheese Muffins

Yields: 8 Servings
Total Macros: 122 Calories| 1.9 g Net Carbs | 9.7 g Protein | 9.1 g Total Fats

Ingredients Needed:

- Almond flour (4 oz.)
- Sea salt (.5 tsp.)
- Cayenne pepper (.25 tsp.)
- Baking soda (.5 tsp.)
- Garlic powder (.5 tsp.)
- Eggs (3)
- Shredded cheddar cheese (6 oz.)
- Grated parmesan cheese (1.5 oz.)

Preparation Instructions:

1. Warm the oven to reach 350° Fahrenheit.
2. Whisk the cayenne, garlic powder, salt, and mix with the eggs.
3. Fold in the baking soda, flour, and each of the cheese options.
4. Stir well and dump the batter into each cup for eight servings.
5. Bake for 25 minutes. Cool slightly before serving.

Cheeseburger Muffins

Yields: 9 Servings
Total Macros: 256 Calories|2.97 g Net Carbs |
19.7 g Total Fats | 14.6 g Protein

Ingredients Needed - Muffin Buns:

- Blanched almond flour (.5 cup)
- Baking powder (1 tsp.)
- Flaxseed meal (.5 cup)
- Salt (.5 tsp.)
- Pepper (.25 tsp.)
- Large eggs (2)
- Sour cream (.25 cup)

Ingredients Needed - Hamburger Filling:

- Ground beef (16 oz.)
- Onion powder (.5 tsp.)
- Salt and pepper (as desired)
- Garlic powder (.5 tsp.)
- Tomato paste (2 tbsp.)

Ingredients Needed - Toppings:

- Mustard (2 tbsp.)
- Reduced sugar ketchup (2 tbsp.)
- Cheddar cheese (.5 cup)
- Baby dill pickles (1 pickle - 18 slices)

Preparation Instructions:

1. Sear the beef in a hot pan with the seasonings.
2. Combine the dry fixings with the wet ones.
3. Warm up the oven to 350° Fahrenheit.
4. Pour into silicone muffin cups. Indent the center to make space for the beef and fill.
5. Bake for 15 to 20 minutes.
6. Remove onto the stovetop and top with cheese.
7. Broil for one to three minutes.
8. Cool for 5 to 10 minutes and remove from the cups before serving.

English Muffins

Yields: 1 Serving
Total Macros: 2.4 g Net Carbs |8 g Total Protein |12 g Total Fats|200 Calories

Ingredients Needed:

- Melted butter or coconut oil (.5 tbsp.)
- Whisked egg (1)
- Unsweetened coconut or almond milk (1 tbsp. or Half & Half)
- Baking powder (.5 tsp.)
- Coconut flour (1 tbsp.)
- *Optional*: Vanilla extract (.125 tsp.)
- *Optional:* Liquid stevia (6 drops)
- Sea Salt (1 pinch if desired)

Preparation Instructions:

1. Warm up the oven to 400° Fahrenheit.
2. Melt the oil or butter in a ramekin.
3. Toss in the remainder of the fixings to the bowl. Stir quickly until the clumps are gone.
4. Prepare in the microwave for 1.5 minutes or bake for 12-15 minutes.
5. Loosen the edges and transfer to a cutting surface. Slice in half sideways.
6. Lightly brown on each side in a skillet prepared with oil or butter. This is a vital step, so don't skip it. Gently press the muffins in the pan with the spatula as they toast.

1-Minute Muffin

Yields: 1 Serving
Total Macros: 377 Calories| 6.3 g Net Carbs| 15 g Total Fats | 8.9 g Protein

Ingredients Needed:

- Almond flour (2 tbsp.)
- Baking powder (.5 tsp.)
- Flaxseed meal (2 tbsp.)
- Salt (1 pinch)
- Oil (1 tsp.)
- Egg (1)

Preparation Instructions:

1. Combine each of the dry fixings. Work in the oil and egg.
2. Microwave for one minute or bake at 350° Fahrenheit for 15 minutes.
3. Serve.

Pesto Egg Muffins

Yields: 10 Servings
Total Macros: 125 Calories|1.2 g Net Carbs |10 g Total Fats |6.9 g Protein

Ingredients Needed:

- Pesto (3 tbsp.)
- Frozen spinach (.66 cup)
- Pitted Kalamata olives (.5 cup)
- Chopped sun-dried tomatoes (.25 cup)
- Large eggs (6)
- Feta - soft goat cheese (4.4 oz.)
- Pepper and salt – Ex. Himalayan salt (to your liking)

Preparation Instructions:

1. Heat up the oven to 350° Fahrenheit.
2. Prep the veggies. Thaw and remove the excess liquid from the spinach or blanch a portion of freshly picked spinach for one minute in boiling water.
3. Transfer the cooked veggies into an ice bath to stop the cooking process. Chop the tomatoes and slice the olives.
4. Whisk in the pesto, salt, and pepper, mixing well. Divide the fixings evenly into the 10 cups– starting with the spinach, cheese, tomatoes, and olives. Blend in the pesto and egg mixture.
5. Bake until browned for approximately 20 to 25 minutes.
6. When the muffins are done, set them on a cooling rack for a short time.
7. You can store the healthy breakfast treats in the fridge for five days or so.

Squash Muffins

Yields: 6 Servings
Total Macros: 3.4 g Net Carbs |111 Calories|7.3 g Protein |7.8 g Total Fats

Ingredients Needed:

- Salt (to your liking)
- Baking powder (.66 tsp.)
- Almond flour (1 cup)
- Peeled & grated squash (1)
- Chopped spring onions (2-3 sprigs)
- Olive oil (1 tbsp.)
- Egg (1)
- Plain yogurt (.25 cup)
- Grated hard cheese (.5 cup)

Preparation Instructions:

1. Warm up the oven to 350° Fahrenheit.
2. Spritz six muffin tins with cooking oil spray.
3. Season the grated squash with salt.
4. Sift the salt, baking powder, and flour.
5. Whisk the egg, and mix with the oil, 1/2 of the cheese, and yogurt. Combine the fixings.
6. Add the squash and juices to the dough. Work in the chopped onions and add to the prepared muffin cups (1/2 full). Sprinkle with the cheese and bake for 25 minutes.
7. Cool slightly and serve. Store in the fridge when cooled - if you have leftovers.

Sweet Muffins

Almond & Apple Muffins

Yields: 12 Servings
Total Macros: 10 g Net Carbs |184 Calories|
5 g Total Protein | 15 g Total Fats

Ingredients Needed:

- Eggs (2)
- Melted butter (.33 cup)
- Maple syrup (4 tbsp.)
- Almond flour (2.5 cups)
- Cinnamon (1 tsp.)
- Thinly sliced apple (1)

Preparation Instructions:

1. Warm up the oven to 350° Fahrenheit.
2. Mix all of the fixings – omitting the apple.
3. Peel and fold the apple slices and pour the dough into the cups.
4. Bake for 15 minutes and cool before storing.

Apple Cinnamon Muffins

Yields: 12 Servings
Total Macros: 3 g Net Carbs |241 Calories| 7 g Total Protein | 22 g Total Fats

Ingredients Needed:

- Nutmeg (1 tsp.)
- Baking powder (1 tsp.)
- Cloves (.25 tsp.)
- Cinnamon (3 tbsp.)
- Almond flour (3 cups)
- Lemon juice (1 tsp.)
- Stevia (to your liking)
- Melted ghee (.5 cup)
- Large whisked eggs (3)
- Applesauce (4 tbsp.)
- *Also Needed:* 12-count muffin tins & paper or silicone cups

Preparation Instructions:

1. Warm up the oven to 350° Fahrenheit.
2. Whisk the dry fixings and blend with the remainder of the fixings in a mixing container.
3. Empty the batter into the muffin pans.
4. Bake for 17 to 20 minutes.
5. Test for doneness by touching the center lightly. If the center springs back, it's done.

Blueberry Flaxseed Muffins

Yields: 10 Servings
Total Macros: 221 Calories|8.78 g Net Carbs|7.57 g Protein |18.33 g Total Fats

Ingredients Needed:

- Flaxseeds (1.5 cups)
- Baking powder (1 tbsp.)
- Eggs (5)
- Vanilla extract (1 tsp.)
- Almond milk (3 tbsp.)
- Coconut oil (4 tbsp.)
- Blueberries (.5 cup)
- Salt (1 pinch)
- Sugar substitute (to your liking)

Preparation Instructions:

1. Warm up the oven to reach 350° Fahrenheit.
2. Use a coffee grinder to prepare the seeds.
3. Combine each of the dry fixings in a mixing container.
4. Whisk the eggs in a mixing container. Pour in the oil and milk. Stir well.
5. Combine all of the fixings - wet and dry.
6. Fold in the berries and stir gently with a spoon.
7. Pour into muffin cups.
8. Bake for 15 minutes. Cool slightly and serve.

Brownie Muffins

Yields: 6 Servings
Total Macros: 183 Calories| 4.4 g Net Carbs |
7 g Total Protein |13 g Total Fats

Ingredients Needed:

- Salt (.5 tsp.)
- Flaxseed meal (1 cup)
- Cocoa powder (.25 cup)
- Cinnamon (1 tbsp.)
- Baking powder (.5 tbsp.)
- Coconut oil (2 tbsp.)
- Large egg (1)
- Sugar-free caramel syrup (.25 cup)
- Vanilla extract (1 tsp.)
- Pumpkin puree (.5 cup)
- Slivered almonds (.5 cup)
- Apple cider vinegar (1 tsp.)

Preparation Instructions:

1. Set the oven temperature to 350° Fahrenheit.
2. Use a deep mixing container to prepare all of the fixings and stir well.
3. Use six paper liners in the muffin tin and add 1/4 cup of batter to each one. Sprinkle several almonds on the tops, pressing gently.
4. Bake approximately 15 minutes or when the top is set.

Cinnamon & Apple Spiced Muffins

Yields: 12 Servings
Total Macros: 198 Calories| 4 g Net Carbs | 7 g Total Protein
|17 g Total Fats

Ingredients Needed:

- Super-fine almond flour (2.5 cups)
- Cinnamon (1 tsp.)
- Sea salt (.5 tsp.)
- Granulated stevia - erythritol blend (.75 cup)
- Baking powder (1 tsp.)
- Large eggs (4)
- Melted coconut oil or butter (.25 cup)
- Vanilla extract (1 tsp.)
- Almond milk – Unsweetened (.25 cup)
- Granny Smith apple (1 – 4 oz.)

Preparation Instructions:

1. Warm up the oven to 350° Fahrenheit.
2. Add liners to a 12-count muffin tin or spritz with some oil.
3. Whisk the stevia, salt, cinnamon, baking powder, and flour in a mixing container.
4. Fold in the coconut oil or butter to make a crumbly mixture.
5. Mix the milk, extract, and eggs in another container.
6. Combine the fixings. Peel, slice and finely dice the apple and add to the batter.
7. Fill each of the cups about 3/4 of the way to the top.
8. Bake until it springs back when gently touched (about 25 to 30 min.).
9. Leave the muffins in the baking tin for 5 to 10 minutes before removing to finish cooling.
10. Serve when cooled or set aside for when you want a delicious snack.

Cinnamon & Applesauce Muffins

Yields: 12 Servings
Total Macros: 3 g Net Carbs |241 Calories| 7 g Total Protein | 22 g Total Fats

Ingredients Needed:

- Melted ghee (.5 cup)
- Large whisked eggs (3)
- Nutmeg (1 tsp.)
- Cinnamon (3 tbsp.)
- Almond flour (3 cups)
- Cloves (.25 tsp.)
- Applesauce (4 tbsp.)
- Baking powder (1 tsp.)
- Stevia (to taste)
- Lemon juice (1 tsp.)
- *Also Needed*: Muffin tins with paper or silicone cups (12-count)

Preparation Instructions:

1. Set the oven temperature to 350° Fahrenheit.
2. Combine the ingredients in a mixing container. Empty the batter into the muffin tins. Bake for about 17 to 20 minutes until the center is springy.
3. Cool before storing.

Lemon Coconut Muffins

Yields: 16 Servings
Total Macros: 2 g Net Carbs | 3 g Total Protein |
7 g Total Fats |78 Calories

Ingredients Needed:

- Erythritol (.25 cup)
- Butter (.25 cup)
- Eggs (3)
- Coconut flour (.25 cup)
- Coconut flakes (.5 cup)
- Baking powder (.5 tsp.)
- Vanilla extract (.5 tsp.)
- Coconut milk (3 tbsp.)
- Lemon - juice & zest (1)

Preparation Instructions:

1. Warm up the oven to 400° Fahrenheit.
2. Lightly grease 16 muffin tins. Whisk the butter and erythritol together until creamy.
3. Break the eggs in one at a time. Add the lemon juice, zest, milk, and vanilla extract. Stir in the baking powder, sifted flour, and flaked coconut.
4. Scoop the dough into the baking pan.
5. Prepare for 20 minutes in the heated oven. Cool slightly and enjoy. Cool thoroughly before storing.

Lemon Poppyseed Muffins

Yields: 12 Servings
Total Macros: 141 Calories|1 g Net Carbs |4 g Total Protein |13 g Total Fats

Ingredients Needed:

- Eggs (3)
- Full-fat ricotta cheese (.25 cup)
- Coconut oil (.25 cup)
- Poppy seeds (2 tbsp.)
- True lemon packets (4)
- Heavy whipping cream (.25 cup)
- Lemon extract (1 tsp.)
- Almond flour (1 cup)
- Swerve or alternative sweetener (.33 cup)
- Baking powder (1 tsp.)

Preparation Instructions:

1. Warm up the oven to 350° Fahrenheit.
2. Prepare a 12-count muffin tin with silicone cupcake liners.
3. Combine all of the fixings until smooth. Scrape the batter into the cups.
4. Bake for 40 minutes. Insert a knife or toothpick in the middle of the muffin to check for doneness.
5. Chill for several minutes before taking them from the liners.

Pumpkin Muffins

Yields: 5 Servings
Total Macros: 3.5 g Net Carbs|185 Calories|7.4 g Protein |
14 g Total Fats

Ingredients Needed:

- Salt (.5 tsp.)
- Baking powder (.5 tsp.)
- Egg (1)
- Apple cider vinegar (1 tbsp.)
- Vanilla extract (1 tbsp.)
- Pumpkin puree (.5 cup)
- Coconut oil (2 tbsp.)
- Sugar-free caramel syrup (.25 cup)
- *Optional:* Crushed almonds (.25 cup)

Preparation Instructions:

1. Warm up the oven to 350° Fahrenheit.
2. Combine all of the components in the recipe list except for the almonds.
3. Prepare a muffin pan for five portions. If you are using the almonds, spritz with some of the oil.
4. Bake for 15 to 18 minutes. Enjoy for breakfast or on-the-go.

Pumpkin Maple Flaxseed Muffins

Yields: 10 Servings
Total Macros: 2 g Net Carbs| 8.5 g Total Fats |
5 g Total Protein|120 Calories

Ingredients Needed:

- Ground flaxseeds (1.25 cups)
- Baking powder (.5 tbsp.)
- Erythritol (.33 cup)
- Cinnamon (1 tbsp.)
- Salt (.5 tsp.)
- Pumpkin pie spice (1 tbsp.)
- Egg (1)
- Coconut oil (2 tbsp.)
- Pure pumpkin puree (1 cup)
- Apple cider vinegar (.5 tsp.)
- Maple syrup (.5 cup)
- Vanilla extract (.5 tsp.)
- *Topping*: Pumpkin seeds

Also Needed:

- Blender such as NutriBullet
- Muffin tin – 10 sections with silicone liners

Preparation Instruction:

1. Heat the oven to 350° Fahrenheit.
2. Prepare the muffin tin with cupcake liners.
3. Toss the seeds into the blender about 1 second – no longer or it could become damp.
4. Combine the dry fixings and whisk until well mixed. Add the puree, vanilla extract, and pumpkin spice along with the maple syrup (.5 tsp.) if using.
5. Blend in the oil, egg, and apple cider vinegar. Combine nuts or any other fold-ins of your choice, but also add the carbs.

6. Scoop the mixture out by the tablespoon into the prepared tins. Garnish with some of the pumpkin seeds. Leave a little space in the top since they will rise.
7. Bake for approximately 20 minutes. They are ready when they are slightly browned. Let them cool a few minutes and add some ghee or butter or some more syrup.

Unflavored Coconut Flour Muffins

Yields: 1 Serving
Total Macros: 113 Calories| 5 g Net Carbs | 6 g Total Fats |
7 g Total Protein

Ingredients Needed:

- Eggs (1)
- Baking powder (.25 tsp.)
- Coconut flour (2 tsp.)
- Salt (1 pinch)

Preparation Instructions:

1. Warm up the oven to 400° Fahrenheit.
2. Grease the muffin cups.
3. Sift the flour and combine all of the fixings. Pour into the cups.
4. Bake for 12 minutes and serve or cool to store.

Delicious Bagels
Almond Mozzarella Bagels

Yields: 6 Servings
Total Macros: 245 Calories| 6 g Net Carbs | 12 g Protein |
 21 g Total Fats

Ingredients Needed:

- Shredded mozzarella (1.5 cups)
- Cream cheese - diced pieces (2 oz.)
- Baking powder (1 tsp.)
- Oat fiber (1 tbsp.)
- Almond flour (1.5 cups)
- Egg (1)

Preparation Instructions:

1. Put the cream cheese and mozzarella in the microwave for 1 minute. Stir and cook for another 30 seconds.
2. Use a food processor to mix the cheese and egg. Work in the dry fixings.
3. Scrap the dough into plastic wrap and put in the freezer for 20 minutes.
4. Warm the oven temperature setting to 400° Fahrenheit.
5. Prepare a baking tin with a sheet of parchment paper.
6. Take the dough from the freezer and shape into six segments. Roll each one into a sausage-shape and form a bagel ring.
7. Place on the paper to bake for 12-15 minutes

Bagels with Cheese

Yields: 6 Servings
Total Macros: 374 Calories| 8 g Net Carbs | 19 g Protein | 31 g Total Fats

Ingredients Needed:

- Baking powder (1 tsp.)
- Almond flour (1.5 cups)
- Shredded mozzarella cheese (2.5 cups)
- Cream cheese (3 oz.)
- Eggs (2)

Preparation Instructions:

1. Set the oven temperature to 400° Fahrenheit.
2. Combine the baking powder, flour, mozzarella, and cream cheese in a mixing container. Place in the microwave to melt for about 1 minute. Stir well.
3. Let the mixture cool and add the eggs. Break apart into six sections and shape into round bagels.
4. *Note*: You can also sprinkle with a seasoning of your choice or pinch of salt if desired.
5. Bake until the edges of the bagels are golden brown (12 to 15 min.).
6. Cool and store.

Cinnamon Raisin Bagels

Yields: 6 Servings
Total Macros: 139 Calories| 6 g Net Carbs | 3 g Protein |
10 g Total Fats

Ingredients Needed:

- Coconut flour sifted (.33 cup)
- Golden flax meal (1.5 tbsp.)
- Baking soda (.5 tsp.)
- Optional: Sea salt (a dash)
- Baking powder (1 tsp.)
- Cinnamon (2 tsp.)
- Whisked eggs (3)
- Unsweetened coconut or almond milk (.33 cup)
- Melted butter - coconut oil or ghee (2.5 tbsp.)
- Liquid stevia (1 tsp.)
- Apple cider vinegar (1 tsp.)
- Optional: Vanilla extract (1 tsp.)
- Golden raisins (.33 cup)

Preparation Instructions:

1. Warm up the oven to 350° Fahrenheit.
2. Grease a donut/bagel pan.
3. Mix the dry fixings (the golden flax meal, the sifted coconut flour, baking soda, cinnamon, baking powder, and sea salt thoroughly.
4. In a separate container, mix the almond/coconut milk, apple cider vinegar, eggs, melted butter/coconut oil, vanilla extract, and stevia.
5. Combine all of the fixings and add to the prepared pan – spreading evenly with a spatula.
6. Bake for 17 to 20 minutes. Set aside to cool for a few minutes. Loosen the bagels with a knife. Turn the bread on the side and slice into half.
7. Serve with a topping of your choice, such as butter or cream cheese.
8. Refrigerate or freeze unused portions.

Garlic Coconut Flour – Gluten-Free Bagels

Yields: 6 Servings
Total Macros: 191 Calories| 3 g Net Carbs | 8 g Protein | 16 g Total Fats

Ingredients Needed:

- Melted butter (.33 cup)
- Garlic powder (1.5 tsp.)
- Sifted coconut flour (.5 cup)
- Eggs (6)
- Salt (.5 tsp.)
- Baking powder (.5 tsp.)
- Optional: Xanthan gum/Guar gum (2 tsp.)
- *Also Needed*: Donut Pan

Preparation Instructions:

1. Grease the donut pan and warm up the oven to 400° Fahrenheit.
2. Mix the butter, garlic powder, eggs, and salt.
3. In another dish, combine the baking powder, coconut flour, and xanthan gum – if you're using it. Whisk the fixings together until the lumps are removed.
4. Spoon into the donut pan. Bake for 15 minutes.
5. Let them cool in the pan (left in the oven) for 10 to 15 minutes. Serve or cool thoroughly before storing.

Homemade Croissant Bagels

Yields: 7 Servings
Total Macros: 83 Calories| 1.1 g Net Carbs | 0.7 g Total Fats|
3.4 g Protein

Ingredients Needed:

- Separated eggs (3)
- Softened cream cheese (2 tbsp.)
- Cream of tartar (.25 tsp.)
- Melted butter (2 tbsp.)
- Sifted coconut flour (2 tbsp.)
- Sweetener of Choice: Erythritol (1.5 tsp.) or Liquid stevia (15 drops)
- Baking soda (.5 tsp.) & Cream of tartar (.25 tsp.) - mixed together
- Sea salt (.125 tsp.)
- *Also Needed*: Donut/bagel pan

Preparation Instructions:

1. Warm up the oven to 300° Fahrenheit.
2. Lightly spritz the pan with cooking oil spray.
3. Separate the egg whites from the yolks.
4. Add the cream of tartar to the egg whites. Whisk using the chosen mixer until stiff peaks form. Sit to the side for now.
5. Beat the egg yolks in another mixing bowl. Combine with the melted butter, cream cheese, the cream of tartar mixture, baking soda, coconut flour, sweetener of choice, and sea salt. Continue beating until the egg yolk mixture is thoroughly incorporated.
6. Gently fold in (do not whisk) all of the mixture and spoon into the pan.
7. Bake for 20 to 25 minutes.
8. Once it's done, remove and cool.

Onion Bagels – Gluten-Free

Yields: 6 Servings
Total Macros: 78 Calories| 1 g Net Carb| 5 g Total Fats |
5 g Protein

Ingredients Needed:

- Coconut flour (2 tbsp.)
- Flaxseed meal (3 tbsp.)
- Baking powder (.5 tsp.)
- Separated eggs (4)
- Dried minced onion (1 tsp.)

Preparation Instructions:

1. Warm the oven to reach 325° Fahrenheit.
2. Mist a donut baking pan with a spritz of cooking oil spray.
3. Sift the coconut flour, flax meal, minced onion, and baking powder.
4. Whip the egg whites until foamy using an electric mixer. Slowly whisk in the yolks and dry mixture. Let the dough thicken for 5 to 10 minutes.
5. Scoop into the molds and sprinkle with a portion of dried onion to your liking.
6. Bake until golden brown or for about 30 minutes.
7. Cool the bagels in the oven.

Pumpkin Bagels

Yields: 8 Servings
Total Macros: 82 Calories| 2.6 g Net Carbs| 5 g Total Fats |
3 g Protein

Ingredients Needed:

- Golden flax meal (3 tbsp.)
- Coconut flour sifted (.33 cup)
- Whisked eggs (3)
- Coconut oil or melted butter (2 tbsp.)
- Unsweetened coconut or almond milk (.25 cup)
- Pure pumpkin puree (.5 cup)
- Pumpkin pie spice (1.25 tsp.)
- Sea salt (.125)
- Cinnamon (.5 tsp.)
- Vanilla extract (1 tsp.)
- Erythritol (1.5 tbsp.)
- Stevia liquid (15 drops)
- Apple cider vinegar (1 tsp.)
- Baking soda (.5 tsp.)

Preparation Instructions:

1. Warm up the oven to 350° Fahrenheit.
2. Generously spritz a bagel or donut pan with the oil.
3. Sift the coconut flour and combine with the cinnamon, golden flax meal, sea salt, and pumpkin pie spice. Stir and set to the side for now.
4. In another mixing container, mix the milk, eggs, sweetener, pumpkin puree, vanilla extract, and melted butter.
5. Whisk the baking soda and vinegar together. Add to the egg mixture. Incorporate everything and stir thoroughly until the batter is smooth.

6. Scoop the batter into the pan forms and spread around evenly. Bake until the tops are browned and firm (about 25 min.).
7. Once it is done, leave it in the pan to cool. You can serve it whole or sliced in half. Refrigerate overnight for firmer bread.
8. Note: Don't use a *pop-up* toaster.
9. Serve with a portion of cream cheese or butter.

Sesame & Poppy Seed Bagels

Yields: 6 Servings
Total Macros: 350 Calories| 5 g Net Carbs | 20 g Protein |
29 g Total Fats

Ingredients Needed:

- Sesame cheese (8 tsp.)
- Poppy seeds (8 tsp.)
- Shredded mozzarella cheese (2.5 cups)
- Baking powder (1 tsp.)
- Almond flour (1.5 cups)
- Large eggs (2)

Preparation Instructions:

1. Set the oven temperature to 400° Fahrenheit.
2. Prepare a baking tray with a layer of parchment paper.
3. Combine the almond flour and baking powder.
4. Melt the mozzarella and cream cheese in a microwave-safe dish for 1 minute, stir, and cook 1 additional minute.
5. Whisk the eggs and add the cheese mixture. Stir and combine with the rest of the fixings. Once the dough is formed, break it apart into six pieces.
6. Stretch the dough and join the ends to form the bagel. Arrange on the baking sheet. Sprinkle with the seed combination.
7. Bake for 15 minutes.

Chapter 4: Ketogenic Buns - Biscuits & Rolls

Buns

Almond Buns for Sandwiches

Yields: 6 Servings
Total Macros: 199 Calories|4.2 g Net Carbs|19 g Total Fats|5.2 g Total Protein

Ingredients Needed:

- Almond flour (1 cup)
- Large eggs (3)
- Butter (2 oz.)
- Salt (1 pinch)
- Baking powder (1 tsp.)

Preparation Instructions:

1. Warm up the oven to 380° Fahrenheit.
2. Add the eggs to a mixing container and whisk.
3. Melt the butter in the microwave or in a pan. Add it to the eggs and whisk.
4. Combine all of the fixings, gently folding by hand.
5. Arrange in the baking pan.
6. Bake for about 15 minutes.

Basil Buns

Yields: 8 Servings
Total Macros: 186 Calories| 1.4 g Net Carbs |9.6 g Protein | 15 g Total Fats

Ingredients Needed:

- Water (.75 cup)
- Butter (6 tbsp.)
- Salt (1 pinch)
- Chopped fresh basil (1 cup)
- Crushed garlic cloves (6)
- Eggs (4)
- Almond flour (.75 cup)
- Grated parmesan (5.5 oz)

Preparation Instructions:

1. Warm up the oven to 400° Fahrenheit.
2. Cover a baking tin with a layer of parchment paper.
3. Boil the water and add the salt and butter.
4. Take the pan away from the heat and add the flour. Combine well and break in the eggs (1 at a time).
5. Fold in the garlic, basil, and lastly, the parmesan.
6. Once it's creamy, add the dough on the prepared pan one spoonful at a time shaping into buns.
7. Bake for 20 minutes and enjoy. Cool before storing.

Breakfast Buns

Yields: 4 Servings
Total Macros: 309 Calories| 4 g Net Carbs | 9.4 g Protein |
26 g Total Fats

Ingredients Needed:

- Whole flax seeds (1 tbsp.)
- Almond flour (.75 cup)
- Baking powder (1 tsp.)
- Psyllium husk powder (2 tbsp.)
- Salt (.5 tsp.)
- Olive oil (2 tbsp.)
- Sour cream (.5 cup)
- Eggs (2)
- Shelled sunflower seeds (1 tbsp.)

Preparation Instructions:

1. Heat up the oven to reach 400° Fahrenheit.
2. Line a cake pan using a sheet of parchment paper.
3. Mix the dry fixings (psyllium, flour, baking powder, salt, and seeds).
4. Combine the eggs, sour cream, oil, and eggs. Fold into the dry fixings. Let it stand for five minutes.
5. Slice the dough into 4 portions and shape into a ball. Arrange the balls in the pan and bake for 20 to 25 minutes.
6. *Tip*: If the dough mixture is still sticky to touch, just use a few drops of oil on your hands while working with the dough.

Burger Buns

Yields: 12 Servings
Total Macros: 3 g Net Carbs|189 Calories|
11.6 g Total Protein |13 g Total Fats

Ingredients Needed - Dry Ingredients:

- Ground sesame or poppy seeds (.5 cup)
- Flax meal (.5 cup)
- Unflavored whey protein/egg white protein powder (.5 cup)
- Almond flour (1 cup)
- Dried oregano (1 tbsp.)
- Coconut flour (1 cup)
- Salt (1 tsp.)
- Minced garlic (1 tbsp.)
- Cream of tartar (1 tbsp.)
- Erythritol (1 tbsp.)
- Baking soda (2 tsp.)

Ingredients Needed - Wet Ingredients:

- Large eggs (2 whole and 6 whites)
- Large egg whites (6)
- Coconut oil - extra-virgin is best (1 tbsp.)
- Hot water (2 cups)

Preparation Instructions:

1. Prepare the oven temperature to 350° Fahrenheit.
2. Toss the sesame seeds in a processor and pulse until powdery. Blend in all of the dry components, omitting the coconut flour for now. Stir well.
3. Mix the hot water and eggs together. Add to the dry fixings, mixing well. Gradually combine the coconut flour until you have a dense uniformity.
4. Scoop the dough onto a baking pan - leaving them several inches apart and sprinkle with the poppy/sesame seeds.
5. Bake for 20 to 30 minutes.

Hot Dog Buns - Almond Flour

Yields: 3 Servings
Total Macros: 274 Calories| 2.7 g Net Carbs|
28.3 g Total Fats | 7.9 g Protein

Ingredients Needed:

- Baking powder (.5 tbsp.)
- Almond flour (6 oz.)
- Eggs (3)
- Salt (1 pinch)
- Oil (4 tbsp.)

Preparation Instructions:

1. Combine and mix all of the fixings. Pour into a microwavable dish.
2. Microwave for 1.5 to 2 minutes. If it's not done cook at 30-second intervals.
3. Slice for the dogs and enjoy.

Hot Dog Deluxe Buns

Yields: 10 Servings
Total Macros: 29 Calories| 1.5 g Net Carbs|
2.1 g Total Fats|1.3 g Protein

Ingredients Needed:

- Almond flour (10 oz.)
- Baking powder (2 tsp.)
- Psyllium husk powder (.33 cup)
- Sea salt (1 tsp.)
- Cider vinegar (2 tsp.)
- Egg whites (3)
- Boiling water (10 oz.)
- *Also Needed*: Parchment paper

Preparation Instructions:

1. Warm up the oven to 350° Fahrenheit.
2. Lightly butter the paper with a portion of butter.
3. Combine each of the dry fixings.
4. Bring the water to a boil.
5. Combine all of the components and prepare the dough.
6. Portion into ten buns and place on the baking tray.
7. Bake for 45 minutes. Serve with your favorite wiener.

Italian Seasoning Buns

Yields: 8 Servings
Total Macros: 2 g Net Carbs | 7 g Total Protein |
20 g Total Fats|26 Calories

Ingredients Needed:

- Eggs (6)
- Flaxseed (1 tbsp.)
- Salt (1 pinch)
- Coconut flour (.5 cup)
- Baking soda (.25 tsp.)
- Melted coconut oil (.5 cup)
- Italian seasoning (.5 to 1 tsp.)

Preparation Instructions:

1. Heat up the oven to 350° Fahrenheit.
2. Mix the coconut oil and eggs.
3. Combine the flour and mix with the salt, baking soda, and Italian seasoning; mixing well until creamy smooth.
4. Leave the dough alone. (Don't knead it for 5 to 10 minutes). At that time, just shape the dough into buns or bread if you prefer.
5. Prepare a baking tin with a sheet of parchment paper. Arrange the bread on the tin and sprinkle with the flaxseeds.
6. Bake for 30 to 40 minutes and enjoy!

Poppy Seed Buns

Yields: 12 Servings
Total Macros: 162 Calories|6.2 g Net Carbs |
11.5 g Total Fats|10.6 g Protein

Ingredients Needed:

- Eggs (6 whites & 2 whole)
- Salt (.5 tsp.)
- Psyllium husk powder (.33 cup)
- Coconut flour (.5 cup)
- Almond flour (2 cups)
- Boiling water (2 cups)
- Cream of tartar (2 tsp.)
- Garlic powder (2 tsp.)
- Baking soda (1 tsp.)
- Poppy seeds (2 tbsp.)

Preparation Instructions:

1. Warm up the oven to reach 350° Fahrenheit.
2. Combine all of the dry fixings.
3. In another dish, add all of the eggs and whisk. Pour in the boiling water and continue stirring.
4. Combine everything and stir until mixed well.
5. Spoon into the pan. Bake for 20 to 25 minutes.

Protein Buns

Yields: 8 Servings
Total Macros: 29 Calories| 0.1 g Net Carbs | 0.3 g Total Fats| 6 g Protein

Ingredients Needed:

- Eggs (2)
- Water (.5 cup)
- Stevia (1 dash)
- Soya protein powder (1.5 or 2 oz.)
- Vanilla extract (.125 tsp.)
- Cinnamon (.125 tsp.)
- Oil for the holders

Preparation Instructions:

1. Warm up the oven to reach 425° Fahrenheit.
2. Prepare 8 silicone cups with a spritz of oil. Whisk the eggs and add the rest of the fixings.
3. Portion the batter into the cups.
4. Bake for 20 minutes.
5. Lower the setting to 340° Fahrenheit.
6. Bake for another 10 to 15 minutes.
7. Cool on a rack briefly and serve.

Sesame Buns

Yields: 12 buns
Total Macros: 133 Calories| 4 g Net Carbs | 7 g Total Protein | 6.5 g Total Fats

Ingredients Needed:

- Baking powder (1 tbsp.)
- Sesame seeds (.5 cup + .5 cup to cover the buns)
- Psyllium powder (.5 cup)
- Coconut flour (1 cup)
- Pumpkin seeds (.5 cup)
- Hot water (1 cup)
- Sea salt (1 tbsp.)
- Egg whites (8)
- Boiling water (1 cup)

Preparation Instructions:

1. Set the oven in advance to warm up to 350° Fahrenheit.
2. Combine the dry fixings. Blend the egg whites in a blender until foamy. Combine them in a food processor until crumbly.
3. Pour in the water and stir to create a smoother dough. Make 12 buns.
4. Empty the additional 1/2 cup sesame seeds in a dish and cover the top side of the bun. Arrange the buns on a parchment paper covered baking sheet.
5. Bake for 50 minutes. For a crunchy top, let the buns cool down in the oven.

Spring Onion Buns

Yields: 6 Servings
Total Macros: 81 Calories| 1.1 g Net Carbs|6.7 g Total Fats|
4.2 g Total Protein

What You Need:

- Separated eggs (3)
- Stevia (1 tsp.)
- Cream cheese (3.5 oz.)
- Baking powder (.5 tsp.)
- Salt (1 pinch)

Ingredients Needed For The Filling:

- Chopped hard-boiled egg (1)
- Diced spring onions (2 sprigs)

Preparation Instructions:

1. Warm up the oven to 300° Fahrenheit.
2. Spritz the muffin cups with some oil.
3. Mix the egg yolks, with the stevia, cream cheese, salt, and baking powder.
4. Whisk the egg whites in another cup. Combine the fixings with a spatula and add the dough into six of the muffin cups (1/2 full).
5. Combine the chopped egg with the onions (filling fixings) and add to the cups. Pour more dough into the cup and bake for 30 minutes.
6. Cool slightly and serve.

Swedish Keto Buns

Yields: 6 Servings
Total Macros: 230 Calories| 5.89 g Net Carbs|7.48 g Protein |20.49 g Fats

Ingredients Needed:

- Large eggs (2)
- Almond flour (1 cup)
- Baking powder (1 tsp.)
- Flaxseeds (2 tbsp.)
- Psyllium husk powder (2 tbsp.)
- Sunflower seeds (1 tbsp.)
- Salt (.25 tsp.)
- Olive oil (2.5 tbsp.)
- *Also Needed:* Parchment paper

Preparation Instructions:

1. Warm up the oven to 380° Fahrenheit.
2. Prepare a baking pan with a layer of paper.
3. Combine all of the dry fixings in a mixing container.
4. Whisk two eggs and add to the sour cream and oil. Mix well.
5. Combine all of the fixings and stir thoroughly.
6. Form the dough using moistened hands.
7. Arrange on the cookie tin and bake for 20 to 25 minutes.

Tahini Hamburger Buns

Yields: 4 Servings
Total Macros: 132 Calories| 4.88 g Net Carbs |5.1 g Protein |10.64 g Total Fats

Ingredients Needed:

- Large egg (1)
- Salt (.25 tsp.)
- Tahini paste (.33 cup)
- Apple cider vinegar (1 tbsp.)
- Baking soda (.5 tsp.)

Preparation Instructions:

1. Warm the oven to reach 350° Fahrenheit.
2. Combine all of the fixings in the blender and pulse until smooth.
3. Layer a cookie sheet with parchment paper and a spritz of oil.
4. Spoon the dough onto the tray.
5. Bake until golden or for about 10 to 15 minutes.
6. Cut into halves and serve.

Biscuits

Almond Flour Biscuits

Yields: 7 Biscuits
Total Macros: 151 Calories| 1.4 g Net Carbs|14.6 g Total Fats
| 3.7 g Protein

Ingredients Needed:

- Almond flour (1 cup)
- Grass-fed ghee - melted (.125 cup)
- Egg (1)
- Salt (.5 tsp.)
- Pepper (.25 tsp.)
- Baking soda (.5 tsp.)
- Garlic powder (.25 tsp.)
- Apple cider vinegar (.5 tbsp.)
- *Optional:* Loosely packed basil (.5 cup) OR Matcha (.5 tsp.) OR your favorite herbs & spices
- *Also Needed*: Parchment paper for lining the pan

Preparation Instructions:

1. Set the temperature setting on the oven to 350° Fahrenheit.
2. Cover a baking sheet with the paper.
3. Combine each of the fixings in a mixing bowl. (If using basil or matcha, blend almond flour, matcha, and basil together in a blender until well combined.)
4. Then, mix in the remainder of the fixings to form the batter.
5. If the mixture doesn't seem doughy enough when you roll it gently in your hands, add in an extra portion of almond meal (1 tbsp. at a time, up to 3 tbsp.) until the dough is workable.
6. Scoop the dough out to form seven balls.

7. Arrange on the baking sheet and flatten each one slightly.
8. Bake until they're golden brown or for 15 minutes.
9. Transfer the biscuits from the oven to the countertop.
10. Serve warm, or cool and store in a covered container to reheat later.

Biscuits & Gravy

Yields: 8 Servings
Total Macros: 5 g Net Carbs|460 Calories| 17 g Total Protein
|40 g Total Fats

Ingredients Needed For The Biscuits:

- Baking powder (1 tsp.)
- Almond flour (1 cup)
- Celtic sea salt (.25 tsp.)
- Egg white (4)
- Organic butter/cold coconut oil (2 tbsp.)
- *Optional:* Garlic or another preferred spice (1 tsp.)

Ingredients Needed For The Gravy:

- Chicken or beef broth (1 cup)
- Cream cheese (1 cup)
- Ground black pepper (1 pinch)
- Celtic sea salt (to your liking)
- Organic crumbled pork sausage (10 oz. pkg.)
- *Also Needed*: Coconut oil cooking spray

Preparation Instructions:

1. Program the oven temperature setting to 400° Fahrenheit.
2. Prepare a muffin pan or cookie sheet with a spritz of cooking oil spray.
3. Cut the butter up into pieces – making sure they are cold.
4. Whisk the whites until fluffy.
5. Sift the flour and baking powder into another container.
6. Cut in the butter and add the salt. Fold in the mixture over the egg whites.
7. Drop the dough onto the baking pan/muffin tin.
8. Bake for 11 to 15 minutes.

Buttery Garlic & Sharp Cheddar Biscuits

Yields: 8 Servings
Total Macros: 144 Calories|0.5 g Net Carbs|13 g Total Fats|6.7 g Total Protein

Ingredients Needed:

- Eggs (4)
- Melted - slightly cooled butter (.25 cup)
- Baking powder (.25 tsp.)
- Sifted coconut flour (.33 cup)
- Salt (.25 tsp.)
- Garlic powder (.25 tsp.)
- Shredded sharp cheddar cheese (1 cup)

Preparation Instructions:

1. Set the oven temperature to 400° Fahrenheit.
2. Cover a baking tin with a sheet of aluminum foil. Grease with a spritz of oil.
3. Whisk the garlic powder, butter, eggs, and salt together. Fold in the baking powder and flour. Whisk until the lumps are removed. Stir in the cheese, mixing well.
4. Drop by the ice cream scoopful onto the baking pan.
5. Bake for about 15 min. Leave it in the pan to cool for 5 to 10 minutes. Remove and serve.
6. *Tip*: They will lose the crispy texture if you don't cool first before you add them to a storage container.

Cheddar Bay Biscuits

Yields: 4 Servings - 8 biscuits – 2 per serving
Total Macros: 2 g Net Carbs | 13 g Total Protein |20 g Total Fats|230 Calories

Ingredients Needed:

- Shredded mozzarella cheese (1.5 cups)
- Cream cheese (.5 of 1 pkg. or 4 oz.)
- Shredded cheddar cheese (1 cup)
- Large eggs (2)
- Almond flour (.66 cup)
- Granulated garlic powder (.5 tsp.)
- Baking powder (4 tsp.)
- Butter – for the pan

Preparation Instructions:

1. Microwave the cream cheese and mozzarella for about 45 seconds using the high-power setting until melted. Stir and return for 20 additional seconds. Stir once more.
2. In another container, combine the eggs with the almond flour, garlic powder, and baking powder. Mix it all together and place on a sheet of flour-dusted plastic wrap. Roll it up into a ball and store in the fridge for 20 to 30 minutes.
3. Heat up the oven to reach 425° Fahrenheit.
4. Prepare a dark color baking dish with butter. Slice the cold dough into eight segments. Place in the prepared pan – leaving a little space between each one.
5. Bake for 10 to 12 minutes.
6. Remove and place on the countertop to cool.

Lavender Biscuits

Yields: 6 Servings
Total Macros: 270 Calories|4 g Net Carbs | 25 g Total Fat|
10 g Total Protein

Ingredients Needed:

- Coconut oil (.33 cup)
- Baking powder (1 tsp.)
- Almond flour (1.5 cups)
- Kosher salt (1 pinch)
- Egg whites (4)
- Culinary grade lavender buds (1 tbsp.)
- Liquid stevia (4 drops)

Preparation Instructions:

1. Warm up the oven until it reaches 350° Fahrenheit.
2. Spritz a baking sheet with a little coconut oil. Mix the coconut oil and almond flour in a container until it's in pea-sized pieces. (It's easier to use your hands.) Set the bowl aside in the fridge.
3. Whisk the eggs until they start foaming. Toss in the salt, lavender, and baking powder. Stir well and mix in the eggs. Add to the almond mixture, stirring well.
4. Place the chunks onto the baking sheet using an ice cream scoop or tablespoon. Pat them, so they aren't round (similar to a pancake).
5. Bake for 20 minutes and enjoy.

30-Minute Drop Biscuits

Yields: 6 Servings
Total Macros: 290 Calories|3 g Net Carbs | g Protein |
30 g Total Fats

Ingredients Needed:

- Egg (1)
- Grass-fed butter (8 tbsp.) or Ghee/coconut oil (7 tbsp.)
- Water (2 tbsp.)
- Apple cider vinegar (1 tbsp.)
- Almond flour (1 cup)
- Coconut flour (3 tbsp.)
- Golden flaxseed meal or psyllium husk - finely ground (5 tbsp.)
- Whey protein isolate (.33 cup) or more almond flour
- Baking powder (3.5 tsp.)
- Xanthan gum (1 tsp.) or Flaxseed meal (1 tbsp.)
- Kosher salt (.5 tsp.)
- Room-temperature sour cream (.33 cup) or Coconut cream + 2 tsp. Room-temperature apple cider vinegar

Preparation Instructions:

1. Set the oven temperature setting to 450° Fahrenheit.
2. Line a baking tin with a sheet of parchment paper or use a baking mat.
3. Whisk the eggs, the soured coconut cream, water, and apple cider vinegar together for a minute or two. Set aside.
4. Combine the whey protein, almond flour, baking powder, flaxseed meal, coconut flour, xanthan gum (or more flax), and kosher salt into a food processor. Pulse until very thoroughly combined.
5. Pour in the butter. Pulse a few times until pea-sized.

6. Fold in the cream and egg mixture, pulsing until combined. Drop six rounds of dough onto the prepared baking tray.
7. Lightly brush with the melted butter.
8. Bake for 15 to 20 minutes. Let them cool for about ten minutes before serving.
9. They will remain delicious at room temperature for three to four days.

Tomato & Zucchini Biscuits

Yields: 10 Servings
Total Macros: 326 Calories| 7.48 g Net Carbs| 9.1 g Protein | 30.2 g Total Fats

Ingredients Needed:

- Eggs (4)
- Butter (.75 cup)
- Almond milk (.5 cup)
- Cheddar cheese (.5 cup)
- Zucchini (.5 cup)
- Coconut flour (.5 cup)
- Almond flour (2 cups)
- Sun-dried tomatoes (2 tbsp.)
- Baking powder (4 tsp.)
- Salt (.33 tsp.)

Preparation Instructions:

1. Warm up the oven to reach 350° Fahrenheit.
2. Butter a baking pan.
3. Sift or whisk the coconut and almond flour, salt, and baking powder.
4. Whisk the milk, eggs, tomatoes, and melted butter.
5. Combine the fixings and process well.
6. Shred and squeeze the moisture from the zucchini. Stir in the grated cheese. Combine and shape into ten biscuits.
7. Toss into the pan.
8. Bake for 20 to 25 minutes.

White Cheddar Sausage Breakfast Biscuits

Yields: 8 Servings
Total Macros: 321 Calories| 3.5 g Net Carbs |13 g Protein |
28 g Total Fats

Ingredients Needed:

- Softened cream cheese (4 oz.)
- Pastured egg (1 large)
- Minced cloves garlic (2 large)
- Chopped fresh chives (1 tbsp.)
- Sea salt (.5 tsp.)
- Italian seasoning (.5 tsp.)
- Blanched cups almond flour (1.5 cups)
- Shredded sharp white or sharp cheddar cheese (1 cup)
- Heavy cream (.25 cup)
- Water (.25 cup)
- Ground sausage, cooked and grease drained (6 oz.)

Preparation Instructions:

1. Set the oven temperature at 350° Fahrenheit.
2. Using a hand mixer on low speed to whip the cream cheese and egg together.
3. Toss in the sea salt, chives, garlic, and Italian seasoning. Add the cheddar cheese, almond flour, water, and heavy cream.
4. Combine until all of the fixings are well incorporated.
5. Fold the sausage into the mixture.
6. Drop the dough in heaping mounds into eight wells of a lightly greased muffin top pan.
7. Bake for 25 minutes.
8. Cool in the pan before removing.

Rolls
Coconut Flour Rolls

Yields: 10 Servings
Total Macros: 102 Calories| 1.3 g Net Carbs | 7 g Total Fats| 3 g Total Protein

Ingredients Needed:

- Coconut flour (.5 cup)
- Psyllium husk powder (2 tbsp.)
- Baking powder (.5 tsp.)
- Pink Himalayan salt (.25 tsp.)
- Water (.75 cup)
- Large eggs (4)
- Butter (4 tbsp.)

Preparation Instructions:

1. Place the oven temperature at 350° Fahrenheit.
2. Combine all of the dry fixings (salt, flour, husk powder, and baking powder).
3. In another container, whisk the eggs with an electric mixer. Pour in the water and melted butter.
4. Slowly combine by adding the dry into the wet components. Shape into ten dinner rolls. Arrange on a silicone baking mat or a greased baking sheet.
5. Bake for 30 to 35 minutes and serve.

Dinner Rolls

Yields: 12 rolls
Total Macros: 3 g Net Carbs|221 Calories| 11 g Total Protein |18.7 g Total Fats

Ingredients Needed:

- Mozzarella cheese (2 cups or 8 oz. pkg.)
- Cream cheese (3 oz.)
- Eggs (2)
- Baking soda (1 tsp.)
- Almond flour (2.5 cups)
- Baking powder (2 tsp.)

Preparation Instructions:

1. Warm up the oven to reach 350° Fahrenheit.
2. Add the cheeses into a microwavable dish and melt. Stir in the eggs.
3. In another container, whisk the baking soda, almond flour, and baking powder. Combine all of the fixings. Blend well with your hands.
4. Prepare 12 balls.
5. Arrange on a greased baking pan. Bake until browned to your preference.

Fathead Rolls

Yields: 4 Servings - 2 each
Total Macros: 160 Calories| 2.5 g Net Carbs |13 g Total Fats|
7 g Total Protein

Ingredients Needed:

- Shredded mozzarella cheese (.75 cup)
- Cream cheese (2 oz. or 4 tbsp.)
- Shredded cheddar cheese (.5 cup)
- Beaten egg (1)
- Garlic powder (.25 tsp.)
- Almond flour (.33 cup)
- Baking powder (2 tsp.)

Preparation Instructions:

1. Heat up the oven to 425° Fahrenheit.
2. Combine the cream cheese and mozzarella. Place in the microwave. Cook for about 20 seconds at a time until the cheese melts.
3. In a separate container, whisk the egg and add the dry fixings.
4. Work in the mozzarella. (The dough will be sticky). Fold in the cheddar cheese.
5. Scoop the dough into a sheet of plastic wrap. Sprinkle the top of the bread with the almond flour.
6. Cover with a layer plastic wrap over the dough. Gently knead it into a ball. Be sure it is covered and place in the fridge for 1/2 hour.
7. Slice the dough ball into four sections and roll each one into a ball. Cut the ball in half which makes the bun.
8. Place the cut side down onto a well-greased sheet pan.
9. Bake for 10 to 12 minutes. Fix them like you like them.

Fiber Bread Rolls

Yields: 11 Servings
Total Macros: 177 Calories| 7 g Net Carbs | 14 g Total Fats|
11 g Protein

Ingredients Needed:

- Almond Flour (1.5 cups)
- Protein (.25 cup)
- Baking powder (4 tsp.)
- Potato or Oat fiber (.75 cup)
- Psyllium husk (3 tbsp.)
- Greek yogurt (1 cup)
- Eggs (4)
- Oil (4 tbsp.)
- Salt (1 tsp.)
- Water (2 tbsp.)
- Vinegar (2 tbsp.)

Preparation Instructions:

1. Warm the oven to reach 300° Fahrenheit.
2. Prepare a baking sheet with parchment paper.
3. Combine each of the dry fixings.
4. Separate the eggs and mix all of the egg whites first. Set aside.
5. Whisk the yolks.
6. Add the yogurt with the wet fixings.
7. Slowly, fold in all of the dry ingredients.
8. Stir in the egg whites and mix gently.
9. Cover the bowl. Let it rest for 30 minutes.
10. Use wet hands to prepare small balls, which you then flatten a bit at the end to make the rolls.
11. Sprinkle with a portion of potato or oat fiber to achieve the white look after baking.
12. Bake for 40 minutes.

Garlic Parmesan Knots

Yields: 8 Servings - 2 each
Total Macros: 220 Calories| 2.66g Net Carbs | 14 g Protein | 16 g Total Fats

Ingredients Needed - Mozzarella Dough:

- Almond flour (.5 cup)
- Coconut flour (.25 cup)
- Baking powder (2 tsp.)
- Garlic powder (.5 tsp.)
- Salt (.25 tsp.)
- Shredded part-skim mozzarella cheese (6 oz. or 1.5 cups)
- Melted butter melted (5 tbsp.)
- Large egg (1)

Ingredients Needed - Parmesan Butter:

- Butter - melted (3 tbsp.)
- Freshly grated parmesan (2 tbsp.)
- Kosher salt (.75 tsp.)
- Minced garlic (2 tsp.)
- Dried parsley (.5 tsp.)

Preparation Instructions for the Dough:

1. Warm up the oven to reach 350° Fahrenheit.
2. Prepare a large baking tin with parchment paper or a silicone liner.
3. Mix the garlic powder, baking powder, almond flour, and salt.
4. In a large saucepan, melt the cheese using low heat until it's melted and stirred together.
5. Fold in the butter and egg.

6. Stir in the almond flour mixture until the dough comes together. It will have a few large streaks of cheese.
7. Turn out the dough onto a parchment-lined surface and knead until uniform.
8. Divide the dough into 16 equal portions.
9. Roll each portion into a 7-inch log. Tie gently into a knot.
10. Place on prepared baking sheet a few inches apart.

Preparation Instructions for the Butter:

1. Whisk the butter, garlic, parmesan, salt, and parsley.
2. Brush about half of the butter over the knots before baking.
3. Bake for 15 to 20 minutes until firm to the touch.
4. Transfer to the stovetop and brush with the rest of the garlic butter.
5. Serve warm.

Keto Bread Rolls

Yields: 6 Servings
Total Macros: 203 Calories|4.7 g Net Carbs|15 g Total Fats|6.2 g Total Protein

Ingredients Needed - Dry Ingredients:

- Almond flour (1.25 cups)
- Coconut flour (.25 cup)
- Ground psyllium husk (.25 cup + 3 tbsp.)
- Salt (.5 tsp.)
- Baking powder (2 tsp.)

Ingredients Needed - Wet Ingredients:

- Apple cider vinegar (2 tsp.)
- Olive (1 tbsp.)
- Hot water (1 cup)

Ingredients Needed - Toppings:

- *Optional*: Sesame seeds (2 tbsp.)

Preparation Instructions:

1. Warm up the oven to 375° Fahrenheit.
2. Prepare a baking tray with parchment paper. Set aside for now.
3. Combine all of the dry fixings first (coconut flour, almond flour, baking powder, ground psyllium husk, and salt). Mix well.
4. Pour in the olive oil and vinegar as well as the hot water. Combine for 1 minute using a spatula. It should remain sticky and soft, but you should be able to form a ball with your hand. If not, just add more husk (1 tsp. at a time). Don't add more than 1 tablespoon of the husk.

5. Set aside 10 minutes to let the fiber absorb the liquid. The dough should be elastic, soft, and easy to divide into six small balls.
6. Roll each small roll between your hands and arrange them on the baking tray. They will not expand while baking.
7. Brush the top of each bread ball with a little tap water. Sprinkle several sesame seeds on top of each bread for a delicious treat.
8. Bake for 40 to 45 minutes.
9. Arrange the tray at the *very bottom* of the oven for .5 hour. Then, swap the pan to the *top* level of the oven for 10 to 15 more minutes.
10. If you love your bread crusty; turn the setting onto the grill mode for an additional five minutes after the baking time. Watch them closely.
11. Thoroughly cool using a wire rack. Slice halfway and enjoy like a bread roll with butter or another tasty treat (add those carbs).
12. Store in the pantry for five to six days. You can store it in a towel to keep them fresh.
13. Rewarm them sliced or in the toaster.

Keto - Paleo Dinner Rolls

Yields: 12 Servings
Total Macros: 74 Calories|2 g Net Carbs | 3g Protein |
5 g Total Fats

Ingredients Needed:

- Organic Psyllium Husk Powder (2 tbsp.)
- Nutiva Organic Coconut Flour (8 tbsp.)
- Finely grated zucchini (1 medium)
- Apple cider vinegar (2 tbsp.)
- Avocado oil (2 tbsp.)
- Large pastured eggs (4)
- Filtered water (.25 cup)
- Dried basil (1 tbsp.)
- Baking powder (3 tbsp.)
- Sea salt (.5 tsp.)

Preparation Instructions:

1. Warm the oven to reach 350° Fahrenheit.
2. Grease a baking sheet.
3. Combine coconut flour, herbs, baking powder, psyllium husk powder, and sea salt.
4. Combine the apple cider vinegar, the eggs, water, avocado oil, and shredded zucchini.
5. Mix the dry ingredients to the wet. Blend with an electric mixer using the medium speed until fully combined.
6. Grease your hands and scoop the dough out by golf ball sized mounds.
7. Gently roll and arrange in the oven.
8. Bake to golden brown and hollow when tapped - approximately 45 minutes depending on size.

Low-Carb Cream Cheese Rolls

Yields: 6 rolls
Total Macros: 91.3 Calories|0.8 g Net Carbs |4.2 g Protein
|8 g Total Fats

Ingredients Needed:

- Large eggs (3)
- Full-fat cream cheese - cubed & cold (3 oz.)
- Cream of tartar (.125 tsp.)
- Salt (.125 tsp.)

Preparation Instructions:

1. Warm up the oven to 300° Fahrenheit.
2. Cover a baking tin with parchment paper. Spritz the pan with cooking oil spray.
3. Carefully, separate the yolks from the eggs and place the whites in a non-greasy container. Whisk with the tartar until stiff.
4. In another container, whisk the salt, cream cheese, and yolks until smooth.
5. Fold in the whites of the eggs, mixing well using a spatula. Mound a scoop of whites over the yolk mixture. Fold together as you rotate the dish. Continue the process until well combined to help eliminate the air bubbles.
6. Portion six large spoons of the mixture onto the prepared pan. Mash the tops with the spatula to slightly flatten.
7. Bake until browned (30 to 40 min.).
8. Cool a few minutes in the pan. Then, carefully arrange them on a wire rack to cool.
9. Store in a zipper-type bag open - just slightly - in the refrigerator for a couple of days for best results.

Oopsie Rolls

Yields: 6 Servings
Total Macros: 91.3 Calories| .8 g Net Carbs | 4.2g Protein | 8.1 g Total Fats

Ingredients Needed:

- Eggs (3 large)
- Cream of tartar (.125 tsp.)
- Softened cream cheese (3 oz.)
- Salt (.125 tsp.)

Preparation Instructions:

1. Warm the oven to reach 300° Fahrenheit.
2. Line a baking tin with a layer of parchment paper. Lightly spray it with non-stick spray.
3. Carefully separate the eggs into clean, non-greasy bowls. Make sure the yolks and whites don't mix.
4. Whisk the cream of tartar and egg whites until stiff.
5. In another container, whisk together the cream cheese, yolks, and salt until smooth.
6. Mix the egg whites into the cream cheese mixture.
7. Scoop into six mounds on the baking sheet. Gently press with a spatula to slightly flatten.
8. Bake for about 30 minutes.
9. Cool and gently transfer the oopsie rolls to a wire rack to cool completely.
10. Oopsie rolls are best eaten on the day they are made. They do not store well.

Rosemary Rolls

Yields: 8 Servings
Total Macros: 89 Calories| 2.3 g Net Carbs | 7.7 g Total Fats|
3.3 g Protein
Ingredients Needed:

- Baking powder (1 tbsp.)
- Almond flour (1 cup)
- Dried chives (1 tsp.)
- Fresh rosemary (2 tsp.)
- Cream cheese (4 oz.)
- Shredded mozzarella cheese (.75 cup)
- Egg (1)
- Butter: For the pan

Preparation Instructions:

1. Warm up the oven to 320° Fahrenheit.
2. Prepare a baking tray with a layer of parchment paper. Spread the surface with a layer of butter.
3. Combine each of the dry fixings (chives, rosemary, flour, and baking powder).
4. Microwave the cream cheese and mozzarella for one minute. Whisk and add the egg.
5. Fold in the ingredients well to form the dough.
6. Cool in the freezer for 15 minutes.
7. At that time, oil your hands and prepare eight small balls of dough.
8. Bake for 20 minutes.

Chapter 5: Ketogenic Sandwiches

Bread for Sandwiches
Cheese Flatbread

Yields: 5 Servings
Total Macros: 170 Calories|5 g Net Carbs| 11.3 g Total Fats|12.3 g Protein

Ingredients Needed:

- Warm buttermilk (1 cup)
- Sifted almond flour (2 cups)
- Grated hard cheese (5.5 oz.)
- Baking powder (.5 tsp.)
- Salt (1 pinch)

Preparation Instructions:

1. Warm up the oven to 350° Fahrenheit.
2. Prepare a baking tin with a sheet of parchment paper.
3. Mix the buttermilk with the salt and baking powder.
4. Grate the cheese and combine with the flour. Mix all of the fixings and knead.
5. Make five balls and add them onto the prepared tray.
6. Flatten into five flatbreads and bake for 15 minutes.
7. Flip once and cook five more minutes. Serve hot.

Delicious Flatbread

Yields: 6 Servings
Total Macros: 70 Calories| 1.8 g Net Carbs | 2 g Protein |
6.6 g Total Fats

Ingredients Needed:

- Butter (1 tbsp.)
- Salt (1 pinch)
- Sifted almond flour (8 tbsp.)
- Water (1 cup)

Preparation Instructions:

1. Sift the flour and add the salt. Cut in the butter. Pour in the water and knead the dough. Let it rest 15 minutes.
2. Warm up the oven to 350° Fahrenheit.
3. Line the baking sheet with parchment and flatten the dough making several flatbreads.
4. Bake for 15 minutes and flip over the bread and bake for another 5 minutes.
5. Remove from the pan and enjoy.

Focaccia Bread

Yields: 9 Servings
Total Macros: 245 Calories | 3.47 g Net Carbs |
10.29 g Protein |20 g Total Fats

Ingredients Needed:

- Almond flour (1 cup)
- Flaxseed meal (1 cup)
- Salt (1 tsp.)
- Large eggs (7)
- Olive oil (.25 cup)
- Baking powder (1.5 tbsp.)
- Minced garlic (2 tsp.)
- Rosemary (1 tsp.)
- 1 teaspoon red chili flakes (1 tsp.)
- *Also Needed*: 9x9 baking pan

Preparation Instructions:

1. Set the oven temperature setting at 350° Fahrenheit.
2. Lightly grease the baking pan. Combine all of the dry fixings and mix well.
3. Use a hand mixer and fold in the garlic and two eggs at a time to reach a dough-type consistency.
4. Lastly, pour in the olive oil mixing well until everything is combined.
5. Put the dough into the prepared baking pan.
6. Bake for 25 minutes.
7. Let cool for 10 minutes and remove from the pan.
8. Cut into squares and cut the squares in half.
9. Add your favorite fixings to the middle!

Keto Naan Bread

Yields: 6 Servings
Total Macros: 370 Calories| 6 g Net Carbs| 28 g Total Fats |
22 g Protein

Ingredients Needed:

- Mozzarella (3 cups)
- Full-fat Greek yogurt (2 tbsp.)
- Eggs (2 large)
- Blanched almond flour (1.5 cups)
- Gluten-free baking powder (1 tbsp.)
- Butter (2 tbsp.)
- Garlic powder (.5 tsp.)
- Fresh parsley (1 tbsp. chopped)

Preparation Instructions:

1. Warm up the oven to 375° Fahrenheit.
2. Layer an extra large baking sheet with a sheet of parchment paper.
3. Mix the yogurt and shredded mozzarella in a large bowl.
4. Microwave for 2 to 3 minutes. Stir every 30 seconds until melted and stirrable. Stir again at the end until well incorporated. (You can also use a double boiler on the stovetop.)
5. Stir together the almond flour, baking powder, and eggs.
6. Working quickly while the cheese is hot and combine the flour mixture to the cheese mixture. Knead with your hands to prepare a uniform dough forms.
7. Shape the dough into a ball. If it's sticky, chill in the fridge for about 15 minutes, until cool to the touch but not frigid cold. (Use this option if it's too sticky to work with.)

8. Divide the dough ball into six sections. Take one piece and shape into a flatbread shape, approximately 1/4 inch thick.
9. Bake the naan for about 8 to 11 minutes, until a few golden brown spots form, but slightly before it looks fully done. If any bubbles form, pop them with a fork to flatten.
10. Whisk the butter with garlic powder, and fresh parsley. Brush over the naan.
11. Return the naan to the oven to bake for approximately two more minutes.

Pita Bread

Yields: 8 Servings
Total Macros: 73 Calories| 1.6 g Net Carbs | 2 g Total Protein |6.9 g Total Fats

Ingredients Needed:

- Sifted almond flour (2 cups)
- Water (.5 cup)
- Olive oil (2 tbsp.)
- Black cumin (1 tsp.)
- Salt (1 pinch)

Preparation Instructions:

1. Heat up the oven setting to 400° Fahrenheit.
2. Prepare a baking tin with paper.
3. Whisk the salt with the flour. Work in the water and oil.
4. Knead the dough and let it rest for 15 minutes.
5. Shape the dough into eight balls. Arrange the prepared dough balls on the paper-lined pan and flatten.
6. Sprinkle with the cumin and bake for 15 minutes.

Other Sandwiches

Keto Grilled Cheese Sandwiches

Yields: 2 Servings
Total Macros: 520 Calories| 5 g Net Carbs |116 g Protein | 46 g Total Fats

Ingredients Needed:

- Unsalted butter - divided (5 tbsp.)
- Whole milk - divided (4 tbsp.)
- Eggs - divided (2 large)
- Salt - divided (.25 tsp.)
- Coconut flour - divided (4 tbsp.)
- Baking powder - divided (1 tsp.)
- Sharp cheddar (2 oz.)

Preparation Instructions:

1. Add two tablespoons of butter into the dish. Microwave for about 50 seconds or until melted.
2. Mix in 2 tbsp. of the milk, 1 egg, and 1/8 tsp. salt.
3. Add 2 tbsp. coconut flour and 1/2 tsp. baking powder and mix until thoroughly combined.
4. Microwave the batter for 90 seconds. Allow it to rest for a minute.
5. Then, loosen the edges of the bread from the container. Arrange the bread on a rack to cool. Continue making another slice.
6. Repeat the steps to make a second slice of keto bread.
7. Warm up one tablespoon of the butter in a skillet using the med-low temperature setting.
8. Assemble the sandwich: Place two cheese slices between the keto bread slices you just made.
9. Once the butter foams, place the sandwich in the skillet.

10. Bake until the cheese is melted or three to five minutes on each side using medium-low heat.
11. Press on the sandwich with a large spatula.
12. Put the keto grilled cheese sandwich on a platter and slice into two triangles and serve.

90-Second Bread with Almond Flour

Yields: 2 Slices
Total Macros: 150 Calories| 1 g Net Carbs | 5 g Protein | 13 g Total Fats

Ingredients Needed:

- Butter - ghee or coconut oil for dairy-free (1 tbsp.)
- Blanched almond flour (3 tbsp.)
- Psyllium husk powder (1 tsp.)
- Baking powder - Gluten-free (.5 tsp.)
- Sea salt (1 pinch)
- Egg (1 large)

Preparation Instructions:

1. Melt the butter, ghee, or coconut oil in a small glass rectangular container.
2. Meanwhile, in a small mixing container, stir together the baking powder, psyllium husk powder, almond flour, and sea salt.
3. Fold the flour mixture into the melted butter.
4. Whisk in the egg and stir everything together until smooth.
5. *Microwave Method:* Microwave for about 90 seconds or until firm.
6. *Oven Method:* Bake for about 15 minutes at 350° Fahrenheit or until firm.
7. Run a knife along the edges, and then flip onto a plate or paper towel to release.
8. Cut in half to form two thick slices. You can slice each piece in half for thinner slices if desired.
9. Toast in a toaster for best results (highly recommended).

Pancake Sandwich

Yields: 1 Serving
Total Macros: 698 Calories| 3.09 g Net Carbs |41.9 g Protein | 55 g Total Fats

Ingredients Needed - The Pancake Bun:

- Pork rinds (0.75 ounces)
- Almond flour (1 tbsp.)
- Beaten egg (1 large)
- Heavy cream (1 tbsp.)
- Keto-friendly Maple syrup (2 tbsp.)
- Vanilla extract (.25 tsp.)

Ingredients Needed - The Filling:

- Hot sausage (2 oz.)
- Large egg (1)
- Cheddar cheese (1 slice)

Preparation Instructions:

1. Add two ounces of the sausage in a silicone ring mold.
2. Use the medium-heat setting to cook until it is medium-well done. Set aside in sheet of heavy-duty foil when done.
3. Crush the pork rinds in a food processor to form a powder. Mix in with the rest of the bun fixings.
4. Fill a ring mold in a pan with half of the batter. Cook on one side until browned, then remove mold.
5. Flip to cook the other side.
6. Add an egg to the ring mold and scramble lightly. Cook until solid
7. Assemble the sandwich and serve.

Chapter 6: Ketogenic Sweet Bread

Banana Bread

Yields: 16 Servings
Total Macros: 8 g Net Carbs | 165 Calories| 4 g Total Protein | 15 g Total Fats

Ingredients Needed:

- Baking powder (1 tsp.)
- Stevia (.25 tsp.)
- Salt (.5 tsp.)
- Xanthan gum (.5 tsp.)
- Almond flour (.75 cup)
- Coconut flour (.33 cup)
- Vanilla extract (1 tsp.)
- Medium eggs (6)
- Erythritol (.5 cup)
- Coconut oil (3 tbsp.)
- Medium banana (1)
- Melted butter (.5 cup)

Preparation Instructions:

1. Warm up the oven to reach 325° Fahrenheit.
2. Grease a loaf pan.
3. Combine the almond and coconut flour with the xanthan gum, stevia, salt, erythritol, and baking powder.
4. Slice the banana and add to a food processor with the butter, oil, eggs, and vanilla extract. Pulse for 1 minute and combine with the rest of the fixings. Pulse for 1 additional minute until well-blended.
5. Empty into the pan.
6. Bake for 1 hr. 15 min. Serve when the urge strikes.

Blueberry English Muffin Bread Loaf

Yields: 12 Servings
Total Macros: 156 Calories| 3 g Net Carbs |5 g Protein |
13 g Total Fats

Ingredients Needed:

- Almond butter - cashew or peanut butter (.5 cup)
- Butter ghee or coconut oil (.25 cup)
- Almond flour (.5 cup)
- Salt (.5 tsp.)
- Baking powder (2 tsp.)
- Almond milk unsweetened (.5 cup)
- Eggs (5)
- Blueberries (.5 cup)

Preparation Instructions:

1. Warm up the oven to 350° Fahrenheit.
2. Prepare a loaf pan with parchment paper and lightly grease the parchment paper as well.
3. In the microwave, melt the nut butter and butter together for 30 seconds in a microwave-safe container. Stir until combined well.
4. Sift or whisk the salt, almond flour, and baking powder together. Pour the nut butter mixture into the large bowl and stir to combine.
5. Whisk the eggs and almond milk together. Pour into the bowl and stir well.
6. Drop in fresh blueberries or break apart frozen blueberries and gently stir into the batter.
7. Scoop the batter into the loaf pan.
8. Bake for 45 minutes or until a toothpick inserted in the center comes out clean.
9. Cool for about half of an hour before removing from the pan.
10. Slice and toast each slice before serving.

Chocolate Zucchini Bread

Yields: 12 Servings
Total Macros: 185 Calories|3.4 g Net Carbs |4.9 g Protein | 17 g Total Fats

Dry Ingredients Needed:

- Almond flour (1.5 cups)
- Unsweetened cocoa powder (.25 cup)
- Baking soda (1.5 tsp.)
- Sea salt (.25 tsp.)
- Ground cinnamon (2 tsp.)
- Sugar-free crystal sweetener (Monk fruit or Erythritol) (.5 cup) OR coconut sugar if refined sugar-free

Wet Ingredients Needed:

- Zucchini, finely grated measure packed, discard juice/liquid if there is any (1 cup or about 2 small)
- Egg (1 large)
- Canned coconut cream (.25 cup + 2 tbsp.)
- Extra-virgin coconut oil - melted (.25 cup)
- Vanilla extract (1 tsp.)
- Apple cider vinegar (1 tsp.)

Optional Filling Ingredients Needed:

- Sugar-free chocolate chips (.5 cup)
- Chopped walnuts or nuts you like (.5 cup)

Also Needed: 9x5-inch baking dish & parchment paper

Preparation Instructions:

1. Warm up the oven to 375° Fahrenheit.
2. Prepare the loaf pan with the paper.
3. Remove the tips of the zucchinis (skin on).

4. Finely grate the zucchini using a vegetable grater. Be sure to press/pack them firmly for a precise measure. Squeeze out any liquid from the grated zucchini.

5. Whisk or sift all the dry ingredients together (sugar-free crystal sweetener, almond flour, unsweetened cocoa powder, cinnamon, sea salt, and baking soda. Set aside.

6. Add all the wet fixings into the dry fixings (grated zucchini, coconut oil, vanilla, egg, coconut cream, and apple cider vinegar).

7. Stir to combine all of the fixings together.

8. Transfer the batter to the loaf pan.

9. Bake for 50 to 55 minutes

10. *Tip*: You may want to cover the bread loaf with a piece of foil after 40 minutes to avoid the top from darkening too much.

11. The bread will stay slightly moist in the middle and firm up after fully cool down.

12. Cool down for 10 minutes in the loaf pan. Then cool down on a cooling rack until it reaches room temperature. It can take up to four hours as it is thick bread.

13. *Tip*: Don' slice the bread before it reaches room temperature; it will be too soft and fall apart when you slice. For a faster option, cool down 40 minutes at room temperature then pop in the refrigerator for one hour for extra fudgy texture and the bread will be even easier to slice as it firms up.

14. Store in the fridge up to four days in a cake bowl or airtight container.

Cinnamon Almond Flour Bread

Yields: 8 Servings
Total Macros: 221 Calories| 7.6 g Net Carbs|15.4 g Total Fats | 9.3 g Protein

Ingredients Needed:

- Fine blanched almond flour - ex. Bob's Red Mill (2 cups)
- Coconut flour (2 tbsp.)
- Sea salt (.5 tsp.)
- Baking soda (1 tsp.)
- Flaxseed meal or chia meal (.25 cup)
- Eggs (5 whole & 1 egg white)
- Apple cider vinegar or lemon juice (1.5 tsp.)
- Keto-friendly maple syrup (2 tbsp.)
- Melted clarified butter or Coconut oil - divided (2–3 tbsp.)
- Cinnamon (1 tbsp. + extra for topping)
- *Optional*: Chia seeds
- *Also Needed*: 8x4 bread pan & parchment paper

Preparation Instructions:

1. Set the temperature in the oven to 350° Fahrenheit.
2. Line the pan with paper in the bottom and grease the sides.
3. Combine the dry fixings (only .5 tbsp. of cinnamon). Set aside.
4. Whisk all of the eggs and blend in the vinegar, maple syrup, and melted butter (1.5 to 2 tbsp).
5. Mix all of the fixings together, making sure to remove any clumps and add to the pan.
6. Bake for 30 to 35 minutes until a toothpick inserted into the center of the loaf comes out clean.
7. Melt the butter and mix it with 0.5 tbsp of cinnamon and brush on top of your bread.
8. Serve or store for later.

Cranberry Bread - Gluten-Free

Yields: 12 Servings
Total Macros: 179 Calories| 4.7 g Net Carbs | 6.4 g Protein |15 g Total Fats

Ingredients Needed:

- Almond flour (2 cups)
- Powdered erythritol or Swerve (.5 cup)
- Steviva stevia powder (.5 tsp.)
- Baking powder (1.5 tsp.)
- Baking soda (.5 tsp.)
- Salt (1 tsp.)
- Unsalted butter melted or coconut oil (4 tbsp.)
- Eggs at room temperature (4 large)
- Coconut milk (.5 cup)
- Cranberries (12 oz. bag)
- *Optional*: Blackstrap molasses (1 tsp.)
- *Also Needed*: 9x5-inch loaf pan

Preparation Instructions:

1. Set the oven temperature to 350° Fahrenheit.
2. Lightly grease the pan and set aside.
3. Sift the flour, baking soda, erythritol or stevia, baking powder, and salt.
4. In another container, combine the eggs, butter, molasses, and coconut milk.
5. Combine it all until well combined.
6. Fold in the cranberries and add to the pan.
7. Bake for about 1 hour and 15 minutes.
8. Transfer the pan to a wire rack to cool (15 min.) before removing from the pan.

Italian Christmas Bread - Gluten-Free

Yields: 7 Servings
Total Macros: 312 Calories| 4 g Net Carbs |10 g Protein | 26 g Total Fats

Ingredients Needed For The Rolls:

- Active dry yeast (1 tbsp.)
- *Optional*: Ground ginger - to help proof the yeast (1 pinch)
- Inulin (1 tbsp.) or maple syrup - to feed the yeast
- Lukewarm water - between 105° Fahrenheit to 110° Fahrenheit (3 tbsp.)
- Sour cream (.25 cup)
- Almond flour * (1.75 cups)
- Whey protein isolate (5 tbsp.)
- Golden flaxseed meal - finely ground (.75 cup)
- Psyllium husk finely ground (2 tbsp.)
- Erythritol or allulose (.66 cup)
- Xanthan gum (2 tsp.)
- Baking powder (2 tsp.)
- Kosher salt (1 tsp.)
- Room-temperature eggs (3)
- Apple cider vinegar (1 tbsp.)
- Orange zest (1-2 tbsp.)
- Unsalted grass-fed butter (.25 cup)

**If paleo or in keto maintenance, sub ¼ to 1/2 cup of almond flour with arrowroot flour for a lighter crumb.

Preparation Instructions:

1. Add a dash of ginger and the yeast to a mixing bowl and set aside.
2. Mix the inulin or maple syrup with the water and sour cream. Heat up over a water bath to 110° Fahrenheit or only feel slightly warm to touch.

3. Pour the room-temperature sour cream mixture over the yeast. Cover the bowl with a towel to rest for seven minutes.

4. Mix both types of flour while the yeast is proofing. Add the whey protein powder, almond flour, flaxseed meal, xanthan gum, sweetener, baking powder, and salt to another dish and whisk until thoroughly mixed.

5. Once the yeast is proofed, add in the vinegar, eggs, and orange zest. Mix well using an electric mixer until fully mixed.

6. Working quickly, fold in the flour mixture in three parts, alternating with the softened butter. Form the dough into a ball.

7. Spoon the dough onto the mini panettone molds, filling them up roughly two-thirds full.

8. Place on a baking tray, cover with a towel and place in a warm draft-free space for two to three hours until the dough has almost doubled in size (it should reach the top of the mold).

9. Warm up the oven to 400° Fahrenheit while the dough is proofing.

10. Lightly brush the dough with egg wash, being careful to avoid the edges so they're able to rise when baked.

11. Bake for 10 minutes at 400° Fahrenheit and reduce the temperature to 375° Fahrenheit.

12. Bake for another ten minutes and reduce temperature to 350° Fahrenheit. Bake for five to seven minutes. The panettone should be a deep brown when done, but feel free to tent with foil to prevent over browning (around 10 to 12 minutes).

13. Allow to cool on the tray for 20 minutes and transfer to a rack to cool completely.

14. Store for three to five days.

15. Serve at room temperature or slightly warm.

Lemon & Blueberry Bread

Yields: 10 Servings
Total Macros: 207 Calories| 5 g Net Carbs|17 g Total Fats|
9 g Total Protein

Ingredients Needed:

- Blueberries (1 cup)
- Lemon zested (1)
- Vanilla extract (.5 tsp.)
- Lemon extract (1 tbsp.)
- Dairy-free mayonnaise (3 tbsp.)
- Medium egg whites (2)
- Whole large eggs (6)
- Salt (.25 tsp.)
- Baking soda (.5 tsp.)
- Almond flour (2 cups)
- Cream of tartar (1 tsp.)
- Coconut flour (.25 cups)
- Stevia (.75 cups)

Preparation Instructions:

1. Warm up the oven to reach 350° Fahrenheit.
2. Prepare the bread pan with a layer of parchment paper.
3. Whisk the almond flour, baking soda, coconut flour, salt, and stevia. Fold in the egg whites, whole eggs, mayonnaise, lemon and vanilla extracts, and lemon zest. Combine well with an electric mixer.
4. Stir in half of the berries (.5 cup) and add to the prepared pan. Bake for 20 minutes.
5. Top it off with the remainder of the berries when it is through the first baking. Continue baking for an additional 50 minutes.
6. Allow two hours for the cake to cool. Serve any time.

Low-Carb Chocolate Loaf

Yields: 8 Servings
Total Macros: 195 Calories| 17.8 g Total Fats|
2.32 g Net Carbs| 5.72 g Protein

Ingredients Needed:

- Large eggs (6)
- Coconut flour (.75 cup)
- Butter (4 oz.)
- Unsweetened cocoa powder (.33 cup)
- Baking soda (.5 tsp.)
- Baking powder (1 tsp.)
- Salt (1 pinch)
- Sugar substitute (as desired)
- Apple cider vinegar (2 tsp.)
- *Also Needed*: Parchment paper

Preparation Instructions:

1. Warm the oven to reach 350° Fahrenheit.
2. Line the baking pan with the paper.
3. Whisk the eggs and stir in the melted butter.
4. Sift the dry fixings. Pour in the wet mixture and add the vinegar.
5. Stir well and pour into the pan.
6. Bake for 20 to 30 minutes.
7. Serve when tested in the center with a toothpick and it comes out clean.

Peanut Butter Berry Breakfast Loaf

Yields: 8 Servings
Total Macros: 153 Calories| 3.3 g Net Carbs |5.8 g Protein
|13 g Total Fats

Ingredients Needed:

- Peanut butter (.5 cup)
- Grass-fed butter, melted (.25 cup)
- Pastured eggs (5)
- Coconut or almond milk (.5 cup)
- Vanilla extract (1 tsp.)
- Almond flour (.5 cup)
- Swerve sweetener (3 tbsp. or as desired)
- Baking powder (2 tsp.)
- Sea salt (.5 tsp.)
- Frozen mixed berries (.5 cup)
- *Also Needed*: Silicone loaf pan or line a loaf pan with parchment paper

Preparation Instructions:

1. Warm the oven to 350° Fahrenheit.
2. Mix the melted butter with the eggs and peanut butter. Mix well.
3. Pour in the coconut milk and vanilla extract. Stir to combine.
4. Sift or whisk the melted butter, almond flour, sweetener, and sea salt. Mix well.
5. Slowly pour the wet mixture into the dry ingredients. Gently fold the mixed berries into the mixture.
6. Pour the batter evenly into the loaf pan.
7. Bake for 45 minutes to one hour.
8. Remove from the oven and allow to cool before slicing.
9. Pop a couple of slices in the toaster and serve with delicious grass-fed butter.

Pumpkin Bread

Yields: 8 Servings
Total Macros: 311 Calories| 5 g Net Carbs |8 g Total Protein
| 26 g Total Fats

Ingredients Needed:

- Almond flour (1 cup)
- Libby's Canned Pumpkin (1 small can)
- Coconut flour (.5 cup)
- Heavy cream (.5 cup)
- Stevia (.5 cup)
- Melted butter (1 stick)
- Large eggs (4)
- Vanilla (1.5 tsp.)
- Pumpkin Spice (2 tsp)
- Baking powder (.5 tsp.)

Preparation Instructions:

1. Program the oven temperature setting at 350°
   Fahrenheit.
2. Grease the pan with some coconut oil.
3. Mix each of the fixings in a mixing container until
   light and fluffy.
4. Empty the batter into the pan. Set a timer for 70 to 90
   minutes.
5. Transfer to the counter to cool before serving.

Seedy Pumpkin Bread

Yields: 8 Servings
Total Macros: 12 g Net Carbs |212 Calories| 9 g Total Protein
| 16 g Total Fats

Ingredients Needed:

- Pumpkin seeds (.25 cup)
- Sesame seeds (.25 cup)
- Sunflower seeds (.25 cup)
- Sugar-free pumpkin puree – canned (1 cup)
- Melted ghee (.25 cup)
- Eggs (4)
- Apple cider vinegar (1 tsp.)
- Almond flour (3 cups)
- Baking soda (1 tsp.)
- Coconut flour (.5 cup)
- Coconut sugar (.25 cup)
- Pumpkin spice (1 tsp.)
- Ground black pepper (1 pinch)
- Sea salt (1 tsp.)
- Chopped rosemary (2 tbsp.)
- Freshly chopped thyme (1 tbsp.)
- *Also Needed:* Loaf Pan

Preparation Instructions:

1. Cover the pan with parchment paper.
2. Set the oven temperature to 350° Fahrenheit.
3. Use a cast iron skillet to toast the sunflower seeds, pumpkin seeds, and sesame seeds, frequently stirring until they begin to release an aroma and brown slightly. Transfer to a flat surface and place to the side for now.
4. In a mixing container, mix the eggs, pumpkin, ghee, apple cider vinegar.

5. In another container, combine the dry fixings (baking soda, coconut flour, pumpkin spice, almond flour, pepper, and salt).

6. Add the dry ingredients into the wet and gently mix. Fold in about 3/4 of the seeds, and the rosemary and thyme. Pour the batter into lined pan and top with the remaining seeds.

7. Bake for 45 to 55 minute - checking the center at 45 minutes with a knife or toothpick.

8. Let it cool completely. Then, slice it into 12 portions. Serve warm with ghee or any other way you prefer.

Slow-Cooked Gingerbread

Yields: 10 Servings
Total Macros: 8.6 g Net Carbs|223 Calories|
9 g Total Protein|25 g Total Fats

Ingredients Needed:

- Almond or sunflower seed flour (2.25 cups)
- Coconut flour (2 tbsp.)
- Swerve sweetener (.75 cup)
- Ground ginger (1.5 tbsp.)
- Dark cocoa powder (1 tbsp.)
- Ground cinnamon (.5 tbsp.)
- Salt (.25 tsp.)
- Baking powder (2 tsp.)
- Ground cloves (.5 tsp.)
- Melted butter (.5 cup)
- Water or almond milk (.66 cup)
- Large eggs (4)
- Freshly squeezed lemon juice (1 tbsp.)
- Vanilla extract (1 tsp.)
- *Suggested Size Cooker*: 6-quarts

Preparation Instructions:

1. Prepare the cooker with a portion of cooking spray or oil.
2. Whisk all of the flour, salt, cloves, baking powder, ginger, cinnamon, sweetener, and cocoa powder in a mixing bowl.
3. Blend in the melted butter, eggs, almond milk/water, vanilla extract, and lemon juice.
4. Empty the batter into the slow cooker and cook until set - approximately
   2.5 to 3 hours.
5. Garnish as desired and enjoy, but count those carbs.

Slow-Cooked Zucchini Bread

Yields: 12 Servings
Total Macros: 13.8 g Net Carbs|174 Calories|
5 g Total Protein |16 g Total Fats

Ingredients Needed:

Preparation Instructions:

1. Combine the coconut and almond flour, salt, baking soda and powder, xanthan gum, and cinnamon. Set aside for now.
2. Mix the oil, eggs, vanilla, and sugar in another dish. Combine the fixings.
3. Blend in the nuts and shredded zucchini. Scoop the mixture into the prepared bread pan.
4. Arrange the cooker on the top rack (or on crunched up aluminum foil balls). You want it at least 1/2-inch from the bottom of the slow cooker.
5. Secure the top tightly. Cook for three hours on the high setting.
6. Cool and wrap the bread in a sheet of foil. It's best when refrigerated.

Chapter 7: Ketogenic Cookies

Amaretti Cookies
Yields: 16 Servings
Total Macros: 86 Calories| 1 g Net Carbs | 8 g Total Fats|
2.5 g Total Protein

Ingredients Needed:

- Coconut flour (2 tbsp.)
- Erythritol (.5 cup)
- Cinnamon (.25 tsp.)
- Salt (.5 tsp.)
- Baking powder (.5 tsp.)
- Almond flour (1 cup)
- Eggs (2)
- Almond extract (.5 tsp.)
- Vanilla extract (.5 tsp.)
- Coconut oil (4 tbsp.)
- Sugar-free jam (2 tbsp.)
- Shredded coconut (1 tbsp.)

Preparation Instructions:

1. Cover a baking tin with a sheet of parchment paper. Warm up the oven to reach 400° Fahrenheit.
2. Sift the flour and combine all of the dry fixings. After combined, work in the wet ones. Shape into 16 cookies. Make a dent in the center of each one. Bake for 15 to 17 minutes.
3. Let them cool a few minutes before adding a dab of jam to each one and a sprinkle of the coconut bits.

Chocolate Chip Cookies

Yields: 24 Servings
Total Macros: 90 Calories| 2 g Net Carbs | 2 g Total Protein
|8 g Total Fats

Ingredients Needed:

- Large egg (1)
- Swerve sweetener (.66 cup)
- Room temperature butter (5.5 tbsp.)
- Vanilla extract (.5 tsp.)
- Almond flour (1.25 cups)
- Sea salt - optional (.125 tsp.)
- Baking powder (1.5 tsp.)
- Coconut flour (1 tbsp.)
- Sugar-free chocolate chips (.5 cup)
- Optional: Molasses (.5 tsp.)
- Optional: Chopped pecans (.25 cup)

Preparation Instructions

1. Use some parchment paper or silicone baking mats to line two baking sheets.
2. Set the oven temperature to 325° Fahrenheit.
3. Use a mixer to blend the sweetener and butter. Stir in the molasses, egg, and vanilla extract until well combined.
4. In another container, combine the two flours, sea salt, and baking powder. Stir until blended. Fold in the pecans and chocolate chips.
5. Arrange the cookie dough by the tablespoonful into the prepared pans. They should be 1.5-inches apart.
6. Bake until the bottoms are browned or about 12 to 15 minutes. Let them cool until firm and set (minimum 25 minutes).

Chocolate Coconut Cookies

Yields: 20 Servings
Total Macros: 1 g Net Carb|77 Calories| 2.2 g Total Protein | 6.8 g Total Fats

Ingredients Needed:

- Almond flour (1 cup)
- Unsweetened shredded coconut (.33 cup)
- Erythritol (.33 cup)
- Baking powder (.5 tsp.)
- Cocoa powder (.25 cup)
- Coconut oil (.25 cup)
- Coconut flour (3 tbsp.)
- Salt (.25 tsp.)
- Vanilla extract (.25 tsp.)
- Un-chilled eggs (2)

Preparation Instructions:

1. Warm up the oven to 350° Fahrenheit. Cover a baking tin with a layer of parchment paper.
2. Mix the dry fixings using a hand mixer.
3. In another bowl, combine the wet ingredients and add to the dry until well blended.
4. Break apart pieces of the cookie dough and roll into 20 balls.
5. Arrange on the cookie sheet and bake for 15 to 20 minutes.

Cinnamon Cookies
Yields: 8 Servings
Total Macros: 260 Calories| 6 g Net Carbs | 25 g Total Fats|
5 g Total Protein

Ingredients Needed:

- Almond meal (2 cups)
- Salted butter (.5 cup)
- Stevia (.5 cup)
- Cinnamon (1 tsp.)
- Vanilla (1 tsp.)

Preparation Instructions:

1. Warm up the oven to reach 300° Fahrenheit.
2. Combine each of the fixings and shape into balls.
3. Prepare a cookie tin with a layer of parchment paper.
4. Arrange the cookies in the pan and press with a fork to flatten.
5. Bake for 20 to 25 minutes.

Ginger Snap Cookies

Yields: 1 Serving
Total Macros: 74 Calories|2.2 g Net Carbs|
6.7 g Total Fats|2.25 g Protein

Ingredients Needed:

- Ground cloves (.25 tsp.)
- Nutmeg (.25 tsp.)
- Salt (.25 tsp.)
- Almond flour (2 cups)
- Ground cinnamon (.5 tsp.)
- Unsalted butter (.25 cup)
- Vanilla extract (1 tsp.)
- Large egg (1)

Preparation Instructions:

1. Warm up the oven temperature to 350° Fahrenheit.
2. Whisk the dry fixings in a mixing bowl. Blend in the rest of the ingredients into the dry mixture using a hand blender. The dough will be stiff.
3. Measure out the dough for each cookie and flatten with a fork or your fingers.
4. Bake for about 9 to 11 minutes or until browned.

Graham Crackers

Yields: 24 Servings

Total Macros: 71 Calories| 1 g Net Carbs | 6 g Total Fats | 1 g Total Protein

Ingredients Needed:

- Baking soda (.5 tsp.)
- Almond flour (2 cups)
- Xanthan gum (.5 tsp.) or Flax meal (1 tsp.)
- Kosher salt (.25 tsp.)
- Cinnamon (1 tsp.)
- Golden erythritol (6 tbsp.) or Pyure (3 tbsp.)
- Butter at room temperature (5.5 tbsp.)
- Egg (1)

Preparation Instructions:

1. Combine the baking soda, flour, salt, cinnamon, and xanthan gum into a mixing container and thoroughly mix. Put to the side.
2. Cream the butter for 2 to 3 minutes using an electric mixer. Mix in the sweetener. Continue beating until light, and much of the sweetener has liquified.
3. Stir in egg, mixing until just mixed. On low, use the mixer and pour in half of your flour mixture. Mix until just incorporated. Mix in the rest.
4. Wrap the dough in plastic. Place in the fridge for a minimum of one hour - up to three days.
5. When ready to bake, warm up the oven to reach 350° Fahrenheit.
6. Roll out the dough until thin. Use a pastry cutter to cut the dough into squares. Place on a parchment paper-lined tray. Store in the freezer for 10 minutes before baking.
7. Bake for 8 to 12 minutes - depending on the thickness and size.
8. Be sure to leave them in the pan for 10 minutes before transferring to a cooling rack. You can store in a closed dish for up to five days.

Macaroons

Yields: 1 Serving
Total Macros: 90 Calories| 4g Net Carbs |2 g Total Protein |
10 g Total Fats

Ingredients Needed:

- Egg whites (4)
- Vanilla (1 tsp.)
- Water (4.5 tsp.)
- Artificial sweetener of choice (1 cup)
- Unsweetened coconut (.5 cup)

Preparation Instructions:

1. Program the oven to 325° Fahrenheit.
2. Whisk the eggs with the liquid ingredients. Stir in the coconut and mix well. Use an immersion blender for uniform consistency.
3. Add the batter into the greased pan.
4. Bake for 15 minutes.

Orange Walnut Cookies
Yields: 10 Servings
Total Macros: 137 Calories|4 g Net Carbs |7 g Total Protein
| 17 g Total Fats

Ingredients Needed:

- Walnut halves (8 oz.)
- Orange - zested (3 tbsp.)
- Stevia drops (20)
- Eggs (1)
- Cinnamon to garnish (1 pinch)
- Shredded coconut - to garnish (as desired)

Preparation Instructions:

1. Set the oven temperature to about 320° Fahrenheit.
2. Toast the walnuts for about 10 minutes until browned. Add them to a food processor. Toss in the rest of the fixings and continue blending until it's smooth.
3. Shape into ten balls and slightly flatten. Drizzle with a portion of the shredded coconut.
4. Bake for 40 minutes. Cool on the rack a few minutes and add to a platter to finish cooling.
5. Store in an airtight container and enjoy any time.

P B & J Cookies

Yields: 6 Servings

Total Macros: 209 Calories| 5 g Net Carbs |9 g Total Protein | 18 g Total Fats

Ingredients Needed:

- Egg (1)
- Creamy keto-friendly peanut butter (.66 cup)
- Stevia sugar substitute (.5 cup)
- Sugar-free strawberry preserves (.33 cup)
- Almond flour (.33 cup)
- Sea salt (.25 tsp.)
- Baking powder (.25 tsp.)
- Pure vanilla extract (.25 tsp.)

Preparation Instructions:

1. Warm up the oven to 350° Fahrenheit.
2. Spray a cookie sheet with a spritz of cooking oil or prepare with a layer of parchment paper.
3. Whisk the egg and combine with the stevia and peanut butter. When it's creamy, add the salt, baking powder, flour, and vanilla.
4. Mix well and shape into small balls. Make an indention in each one and add one teaspoon of preserves.
5. Bake until browned or for about 10 to 12 minutes.
6. Cool on a wire rack and serve.

Pistachio Cookies

Yields: 16 Servings
Total Macros: 135 Calories| 2 g Net Carbs | 12 g Total Fats|
4 g Total Protein

Ingredients Needed:

- Melted butter (6 tbsp.)
- Chopped pistachios (.5 cup)
- Erythritol (.5 cup)
- Almond flour (2 cups)

Preparation Instructions:

1. Mix each of the fixings together in a mixing container.
2. Shape the dough into a long roll and cover with a sheet of plastic wrap.
3. Place in the fridge for about ½ hour. Unwrap and slice into 16 portions.
4. Bake for 12 to 15 minutes.

Walnut Cookies

Yields: 16 Servings
Total Macros: 72 Calories| 1.1 g Net Carbs |
6.7 g Total Fats|3 g Total Protein

Ingredients Needed:

- Egg (1)
- Ground cinnamon (1 tsp.)
- Erythritol (2 tbsp.)
- Ground walnuts (1.5 cups)

Preparation Instructions:

1. Warm up the oven to reach 350° Fahrenheit.
2. Combine the cinnamon and erythritol with the egg.
3. Fold in the walnuts.
4. Shape into balls and place on a parchment paper-lined baking tin.
5. Bake for 10 to 13 minutes.

Conclusion

I hope each segment of the *Keto Diet Bread* was enjoyable. I also hope each chapter was informative and provided you with all of the tools you need to achieve your goals of baking your bread while remaining in ketosis. You will be surprised how quickly the pounds will drop as you enjoy each morsel of the bread, pastries, and cookies!

There's no need to stress since you have all of the nutritional information included with each of the delicious menu suggestions.

The next step is to prepare your shopping list and head out to the store to get all of the fixings for your newest challenge in baking. The step-by-step process will help you through each of the selections.

At the end of a hard day, why not have a delicious mug of cocoa? Here is the recipe:

Hot Chocolate

Yields: 1 Serving

Total Macros: 216 Calories| 1 g Net Carbs|23 g Total Fats |1 g Protein

Ingredients Needed:

- Cocoa powder (1 tbsp.)
- Unsalted butter (1 oz.)
- Vanilla extract (.25 tsp.)
- Boiling water (1 cup)
- Powdered erythritol - optional (1 tsp.)
- *Also Needed*: Immersion blender

Preparation Instructions:

1. Add each of the ingredients into a tall container to prepare using the blender.
2. Mix for about 15 to 20 seconds until the foam is no longer on the top.
3. Pour the cocoa into the cups and serve.

Finally, if you found this book useful in any way, a review on Amazon is always appreciated!

Made in the USA
San Bernardino, CA
10 August 2019